— THE TIPPING POINT

LIFE FORCE COMES FROM QUESTIONING YOUR THOUGHTS

METTE REEBIRK

The Tipping Point:
Life Force Comes From Questioning Your Thoughts

Copyright © 2023 by Mette Reebirk. All rights reserved.

No portion of this book may be reproduced in any form without written permission from the publisher or author, except as permitted by U.S. copyright law.

This publication is designed to provide accurate and authoritative information in regard to the subject matter covered. No representations or warranties with respect to the accuracy or completeness of the contents of this book and no implied warranties of fitness for a particular purpose are made. The advice and strategies contained herein may not be suitable for your situation. You should consult with a professional when appropriate. Neither the publisher nor the author shall be liable for any loss of profit or any other commercial damages, including but not limited to special, incidental, consequential, personal, or other damages.

Book Cover by Diren Yardimli
Cover Photo by Photographer, Rune Hansen

Paperback: 9798370375835
Hardback: 9798370375934

Contents

Introduction 10
How to read this book? 12

CHAPTER 1
Consciousness, the master key 15
Meet your inner roommate 21
What is craziness? 24
You, the expert 27

CHAPTER 2
How do thoughts make up our world? 31
What comes before thoughts? 32
How stressful feelings come about? 40
How emotions are formed 47

CHAPTER 3
Reality is kinder than we think 53
The distinction between reality and fiction 56
Only you are responsible for your happiness 58

Chapter 4
When you give, you receive 63
Let go of any attachments 67
Tell me how you treat others,
and I will tell you who you are 70
Why do we become angry? 73

Chapter 5
Everything is Okay 77
The don't know mind and leadership 78
To be present 80
Meet your teacher 82
When do you know to change? 87

Chapter 6
No one can hurt me but me 91
The oxymorons of life 93
Giving is receiving 96
What is success for you? 99

Chapter 7
How to get rid of stress? 107
What do we think about stress? 108
Most problems arise from misunderstandings .. 112
Being angry makes you believe everything 118

CHAPTER 8
Welcome to earth school 121
Teachers surround us 122
What you don't know, you know 124
Meet your fundamental beliefs 126
We don't own anything 128

CHAPTER 9
Without your story, who are you? 131
There is nothing new, just repetition 136

CHAPTER 10
When nothing is going your way 139
How to win the war against yourselves? 143
To show dignity to yourself 147
Let go 149
Listen with your heart 151

CHAPTER 11
The power of vulnerability 155
Seek, and you shall find happiness 159
Courage to live 162

Chapter 12
Be the difference you want to see 167
Lead from within 169
Playing the wrong role 171
When more than being intelligent is needed 174
Hope - hopelessness - trust 178
Patience - requires some
patience and gratitude 180

Chapter 13
Wake up and become a philosopher 187
It takes one to know one! 190
The blind spot 193

Chapter 14
Follow your intuition 197
It's about right and wrong! 200
Afraid of living 203

Chapter 15
Life and quantum physics 209
Being human and having pure energy 210
Dalai Lama and science 213

CHAPTER 16
What you don't know about the brain 217
The brain is guessing 219
We construct our emotions 220
Brain versus Mind 223

CHAPTER 17
How to train your awareness 229
Be aware of you watching you 230
Meditation 232
Questioning what is hard to question 235
Become a truth seeker 238

CHAPTER 18
Stories to reflect upon 241
How Christian gained a less stressful life 242
Are you sure the elephant is blue? 243
The smart boss learned something new 245
The tipping point 247

CHAPTER 19
One thought from inner peace 251

Acknowledgements 257
Literature 259
About the Author 263

Introduction

When you're caught up in your thoughts, it's easy to forget that thoughts are something you have, not something you are. Once you realize this, you can start to become aware of your thoughts, choose other thoughts and detach from unproductive beliefs causing you pain.

Nobody deserves to live with the feeling that they are at the mercy of their thoughts. But it can be hard to accept the reality. Because there's only one root cause to your struggle, that you allow your mind to run wild and entertain whatever thoughts occur without questioning if they are true or not.

Only when we stop believing the unproductive stories we tell ourselves and meet our thoughts with the curiosity of their truthfulness can we make any progress. The problem is, some of our thoughts and beliefs are so well integrated in our minds they can be hard to discover. Others are so painful to question, we simply don't - even if questioning them is exactly what we need to relieve pain, find new energy, and move past our struggles.

By engaging your curiosity to explore your beliefs truly, you can start uncovering the truth behind them, paving the way for proper growth and change. Taking the plunge may not always be easy, but it promises its rewards.

Three gifts stand out reading the book.

First, Mette teaches you how to confront uncomfortable truths; thereby you will learn how your thoughts shape your perceptions and emotional experience and, thereby, your reality.

Next, she shows you how to inquire deeply into the cause and root of what you believe to be true – seeking to understand the source of any irrational thinking and feelings so you can choose alternative ways to live a kinder life.

Finally, she inspires you to become aware of your habits – old ways of thinking that no longer serve you – so that you can create more beneficial patterns in their place.

With these thoughtful presents in mind, it is up to you to take ownership in cultivating more conscious decision making and healthy relationships with yourselves.

How to read this book?

The book is about how we become aware of our thoughts and stop the mental war we have going on, so we can live friendlier lives.

It starts with you becoming aware of what is holding you back from doing more of what you love because your beliefs about yourself and the world around you are invalid.

Along the way, you will discover that what makes you sad, angry or anxious is based on a story you tell yourself, that is false.

You will experience how you can see through and recognise the unconscious assumptions that bring you out of balance.

I invite you to read the book with an open mind. Your nuggets of gold you can only find through your curiosity and sincere desire to find your own answers.

While reading, you may experience a lot of repetitions that are reframed.

Our understanding of the world around us is often based on patterns and variables we anticipate or discover in new experiences. Only when we are exposed to something in a multitude of contexts can we properly understand its nature and purpose.

To comprehend something means going beyond simply taking it at face value and instead questioning and probing it in different ways, which requires encountering it repeatedly in various settings.

Only then can we start to challenge our initial suppositions, as what could initially seem like one straight forward problem turn out to be an unquestioned thought with more intricate support systems worth exploring.

Be curious about where the reading leads you this will give you the insight you are looking for.

The reason is that we learn individually and to gain insight at a deep inner level, it is not enough to be a clever freshman. Instead, you need to let go of what you believe the truth looks like, be curious about what will emerge when you become still, and make what you read yours.

The ability to question your thoughts and beliefs is essential in finding the peace and happiness you deserve. So go ahead - dive in and enjoy the journey!

CHAPTER 1

Consciousness, the master key

Consciousness refers to our awareness of ourselves and our environment. It's the part of us that allows us to think, feel, and experience the world around us.

Who are you talking to in your head?

Are you talking to yourself? Or are you talking to someone else?

If you're talking to yourself, then who are you? Are you your thoughts? Your feelings?

No, you are not your thoughts or your feelings. However, you are the one who is aware of your thoughts and feelings.

So, if you're talking to yourself in your head, then who are you talking to? Who is this "you" you're talking with in the dialogue you have going in your mind?

You are the one observing the dialogue in your head. You are the one who is aware of your thoughts and feelings.

But wait, there's more! If you're talking to yourself in your head, then who is this "you" observing the chit-chat going on in your head? It's your consciousness.

So, who are you talking to when you're talking to yourself in your head? You are talking to your consciousness.

Michael A. Singer frames it beautifully in his book "The Untethered Soul":

> "You are the one who is having the human experience. You are not the human experience. There is a difference. The "you" that you think you are is only a thought. It's time for that thought to end."

When you're talking to yourself in your head, you're talking to your consciousness. So the next time you find yourself in a never-ending inner dialogue, take a step back and ask yourself: "Who am I talking to?"

Stop and listen to the answer. It might just surprise you.

When you meet something that could eventually upset you, you observe it. You don't attach to it. You just witness it passing through.

You might think, "Oh, this is bad," but immediately recognise that it's just a thought. It's not you.

You are not your thoughts. However, you are the one who is aware of your thoughts.

And once you realize that, you can start to detach from the thoughts that are causing you pain.

You can start to see them for what they are, just thoughts. They don't have any power over you unless you give them power.

So the next time you find yourself in a never-ending inner dialogue, take a step back and ask yourself: "Who am I talking to?"

You don't let it define you because it is something you experience, not something you are. And then, let it go.

Have you ever had a thought so real it almost seemed like an experience?

The way our emotions and thoughts interact causes this natural phenomenon, according to research by prominent researchers like Drs. Joseph Ledoux, and Karim Nader emotions are created as chemistry in the brain's cells. It explains why we "feel" our feelings and thinking: we taste them mixed with our emotions.

Our thoughts activate all of our senses, reinforcing our feelings and creating the sensation that our thoughts are tangible. We can experience this for ourselves if we think about a particular food we enjoy; chances are - even just thinking about it will cause us to salivate or feel pleasant emotions drawing on memories associated with that specific meal. Similarly, negative emotions can also be relieved if we remember something terrible happened while feeling anxiety or fear at that moment. In other words, when your mind is activated in an emotionally charged event or thought - your body responds as if it were happening right now!

Researcher and PhD Lisa Feldman Barrett wrote an excellent book, "How Emotions are Made, " which explains how our thoughts create our emotions.

We will get back to this and look deeper into the science of emotions.

Self-consciousness is the key to freedom. When you're self-conscious, you're aware of your thoughts and emotions as they're happening. Consciousness is, "the state or quality of being aware of and able to think, feel, and perceive."

Being self-conscious allows you to step back and observe your thoughts and emotions without getting caught up in them. It's like watching a movie unfold on a screen; you're aware of what's happening, but you're not part of the story.

Next time you watch a movie, try to be self-conscious. It's more challenging than it sounds!

The reason why it's so challenging to be self-conscious because we're so used to identifying with our thoughts and emotions. We think they are who we are.

But if you take a step back and look at your thoughts and emotions, you'll see that they're just fleeting ideas and feelings that come and go. They're not permanent. We have around seventy thousand thoughts a day. So it's impossible to be our thoughts. Very few people can see the gaps between the thoughts. Imagine thoughts to be like drops of water and the space between like air.

Francesco Varela, a philosopher and neuroscientist, said, "The experience of consciousness is like watching a movie. The images on the screen (the thoughts) come and go, but the space between the images (the conscious awareness) is always there."

Only when we start seeing our thoughts and emotions as temporary visitors can we detach from them. And it's only when we disconnect from our thoughts and feelings we can find some peace and calm in our minds.

The oldest Chinese symbol for consciousness is a drawing of a heart. The heart was considered the seat of consciousness because it was thought to be the organ most affected by our thoughts and emotions. It's said that when we're not self-conscious, our heart is like a turbulent sea tossed about by the waves of our thoughts and feelings. But when we become self-conscious, it's like the sea calms, and we can see again.

Self-consciousness is the key to freedom because it allows us to detach from our thoughts and emotions and see them for what they are: fleeting ideas and feelings that come and go. They don't have any power over us unless we give them energy.

And the more you practice being self-conscious, the easier it becomes. With time, you'll be able to observe your thoughts and emotions without getting caught up in them. And that's when true freedom is experienced.

What is freedom? Freedom is the ability to act, think, and feel without being constrained by your past. Platon described it like this, "If you all your life have been in a cave and then you come out into the sunlight, that's what freedom is."

When you're self-conscious, you're no longer a slave to your thoughts and emotions. You're free to act, think, and feel without being constrained by them. And that's true freedom.

Meet your inner roommate

Michael A. Singer describes our thoughts with a beautiful analogy in his book "The Untethered Soul." He says that our thoughts are like a noisy roommate who we live with. This roommate is always there, making noise and causing trouble. But we've gotten so used to living with this roommate that we don't even realize how much of a nuisance he is!

The first step to becoming self-conscious is to become aware of this noisy roommate. Observe your thoughts without judgment or attachment. Just watch them as they come and go.

The second step is to start setting boundaries with your noisy roommate. Let him know that you're in charge, not him. The more you practice this, the quieter he'll become.

And the third step is to move out of the apartment altogether! It means detaching from your thoughts and emotions entirely. It is when true freedom begins.

So, if you're ready to start living a life of true freedom, self-consciousness is the key. Start by observing your thoughts without judgment or attachment. Then begin setting boundaries with your noisy roommate. Finally, detach from your thoughts and emotions entirely. With time and practice, you'll be able to live a life of true freedom.

Why do we judge everything and everyone?

One of the main reasons why we judge everything and everyone is because we're not self-conscious. We're so used to being controlled by our thoughts and emotions that we don't even realize it!

When we're not self-conscious, our thoughts and emotions rule our lives. We're like a leaf in the wind, blown around by whatever thoughts and feelings come our way.

Has this judging behaviour anything to do with having an ego?

Yes, the ego is one of the main reasons why we judge everything and everyone. The ego is the part of us always trying to protect ourselves from harm. It's the part of us constantly comparing ourselves to others and putting them down to make ourselves feel better.

To chase feeling better means that we do not feel good. We might feel unhappy, contentor fulfilled. So we judge others to make ourselves feel better.

But the problem is, it only makes us feel worse in the long run. It's like a drug that gives us a temporary high but leaves us feeling worse.

The funny part is that when we believe we judge our neighbour, we judge ourselves.

When we judge others, we're simply judging ourselves. We're attacking ourselves with our thoughts and emotions. We're putting ourselves down to make ourselves feel better.

But like I said, this only makes us feel worse in the long run. It's like a drug that gives us a temporary high but leaves us feeling worse.

So if you want to stop judging others, start by looking at your judgments. What are you saying about yourself when you judge someone else?

The only way to truly feel better is to question if what the ego comes up with is the truth, the author Byron Katie says in her book, "Loving What Is."

Byron Katie describes it like this, "The ego is like a teenager who's convinced that life is completely unfair. So it's not interested in hearing anything else."

So if you judge everything and everyone, it's a sign that you're not self-conscious. Instead, you're letting your thoughts and emotions rule your life. And the only way to break free from this is to become self-conscious.

Start by observing your thoughts and emotions without judgment or attachment. Then start setting boundaries for your noisy roommate. And finally, detach from your thoughts and feelings entirely. With time and practice, you'll be able to live a life of true freedom.

What is craziness?

We are all crazy when we believe our thoughts to be true. The author Yuval Noah Harari describes crazy in his book "Sapiens":

"The standard definition of 'crazy' in the Western world is believing something that isn't supported by evidence. A person who believes in Santa

Claus or the Tooth Fairy is considered crazy. So are people who believe in extraterrestrial beings or fairies living at the bottom of the garden."

But what if I told you there's a different kind of craziness?

This craziness is when we believe our thoughts to be reality. We think that our thoughts are true simply because we're thinking them. But just because we're thinking something doesn't make it true.

When we are not self-conscious, thoughts just come and go without notice. We believe them to be accurate and act accordingly.

Craziness is when our actions are not in alignment with what we truly want in life. For example, we might say that we want peace and love, but if our steps are full of judgment and hatred, that's not aligned with our true desires.

When do we know something is more true than something else?

There is no one answer to this question. However, an excellent way to know if something is more authentic than something else, is to ask yourself if it's coming from a place of love or fear.

If it comes from a place of love, it's likely to be true. If it comes from a place of fear, then it's likely to be false.

For example, if you're thinking about quitting your job, a thought that comes from love would be, "I want to quit my job because I'm not happy, and I want to do something that makes me feel good."

A thought that comes from fear would be, "I want to quit my job because I'm scared of failing, and I don't think I can do it."

As you can see, one thought comes from a place of love, and the other comes from a place of fear. The thought coming from love is likely accurate, while the thought coming from fear is likely false.

The only way to know is to listen to your heart and intuition. They will never lead you astray.

Professor Otto Scharmer at MIT has said: "that fear-based thinking is like a virus that infects our minds and prevents us from seeing the truth".

The philosopher Humberto Maturana described the heart and love as the key to seeing the truth. He said, "The heart is the organ of possibility because it is where love resides. Therefore, love is what allows us to see possibility."

When we are self-conscious, we can see things as they are and not through the lens of our ego.

You, the expert

With more self-consciousness, you will better understand yourself and your emotions and love what is. You will see you are the expert yourself.

As the expert, it's your job to observe your thoughts and feelings without judgment or attachment.

Nothing outside of yourself can ever give you what you are looking for.

Remember, a good teacher is also a good student. So to teach someone else, you first must learn the material yourself. The same goes for happiness and peace. You can't give what you don't have.

The world is how you perceive it. The inner and the exterior always fit together - they are one. If you want to change the way you see the world, start by changing the way you see yourself.

Developing greater self-awareness is essential in understanding your thoughts and feelings without judgment or attachment.

Only when we take the time to observe our inner selves can we begin to understand what makes us feel content, fulfilled, or satisfied.

Taking a step back and observing our inner selves can help us understand what makes us happy, fulfilled and content. To do this, we need to create space between our thoughts and emotions to view them objectively. It may be as simple as asking questions that you don't necessarily know the answer to - questions like 'how do I really feel right now?', 'why does this bother me?' or 'in what way am I growing?'.

By asking questions, curiosity over judgment will help you find the answers you are looking for, which may further develop your understanding of yourself.

Once you become aware of your inner self, it's essential to accept it as it is. Don't fight against who you are - instead, try to understand why certain emotions arise within you and how they contribute to making life decisions.

Additionally, focus on building self-confidence by learning more about yourself daily - how you think, feel, and what drives you forward - so that when difficult situations arise, you can deal with them with clarity and stressless.

When we reach this level where we meet people where they are, we become the teacher people want to follow.

It's also important to remember that the inner world reflects the outer world; they are the same! So if changes need to be made externally – such as changing our surroundings – it all starts with making changes internally first, such as challenging our thought processes or being open-minded towards new possibilities within life.

> "The greatest revolution of our generation is the discovery that human beings, by changing the inner attitudes of their minds, can change the outer aspects of their lives."
> - *Psychologist and Philosopher William James.*

Each of us is responsible for our happiness. No one can make us happy but ourselves. And we can't be satisfied if we're not self-conscious. When I take care of myself, I care for those around me. It doesn't work the other way around.

It also means that nobody can do me any harm. It's a privilege only I have. So if someone hurts me, I've allowed them to. It doesn't mean they're terrible; it just means that I need to be more self-conscious about who I allow into my life.

> "You can never hurt me more than I've already hurt myself."
> - *B.B. King.*

CHAPTER 2

How do thoughts make up our world?

The spiritual teacher Echart Tolle defines thought as "a mental event that arises in the form of a picture or a sound or a sensation or a feeling in your head, which you may think is true."

All thoughts are just electrical impulses in the brain. They're not real. And yet, we believe them to be true. We even think our thoughts define who we are. A thought is a mental construct that we create in our minds. Thoughts are not honest; they are just concepts.

PhD Lisa Feldmann Barrett describes thoughts as a prediction our brain makes about the world. Thoughts are not facts; they are just interpretations. Lisa Feldmann explains that our thoughts are just like the weather. The weather is not good or bad; it just is. And our thoughts are the same way. Thoughts are not good or bad; they are.

What comes before thoughts?

There is something that is beyond thoughts. This something is the present moment. The present moment is always perfect, no matter what our thoughts about it are.

The only thing that is real is the present moment. Everything else is just a thought.

And when we are self-conscious, we can see thoughts for what they are: electrical impulses in the brain that are not real.

"A thought is just a guest in your mind; it's not who you are. You are the host." - Anil Seth.

Anil Seth is a British neuroscientist and writer. He is the author of "The Mind Is Flat: The Remarkable Shallowness of Human Psychology".

Four ways thought can enter the mind:

1. through the five senses (sight, sound, smell, taste, and touch),

HOW DO THOUGHTS MAKE UP OUR WORLD?

2. through memories,
3. through imagination, or
4. through thoughts about thoughts (meta-thoughts).

Thoughts about thoughts are the most dangerous because they can create a never-ending loop of thinking. It is what happens when we overthink things. We get stuck in a thinking circle and can't get out.

The only way to break out of this loop is to become self-conscious. When we are self-conscious, we can see thoughts for what they are: electrical impulses in the brain that are not real.

> "You don't have to believe everything your mind tells you. Just because you think something isn't true."
>
> *- Unknown*

How we think about ourselves and the world around us creates our reality.

If we believe that the world is scary, we will see evidence everywhere. We will find stories in the news that confirm our beliefs, and we will attract people into our lives who reflect our fears.

Conversely, if we believe that the world is a good place, we will also find evidence. We will see stories of people helping each other, and we will attract kind and loving people into our lives.

Our reality is a reflection of our innermost thoughts and beliefs.

"You are not a victim of the world but rather a victim of your thoughts. You have the power to change your life by changing your thoughts." - Wayne Dyer was an American self-help author and motivational speaker.

The first step to changing our thoughts is to become aware of them. After that, we can only change what we're aware of.

When we are self-conscious, we can see thoughts for what they are: electrical impulses in the brain that are not real. We can then choose which thoughts to believe and which to ignore.

For example, if I believe I need to improve, I will find evidence everywhere I look. I will see how I am not good enough, and I will attract people into my life who reflect on my feelings of inadequacy.

Conversely, I will also find evidence if I believe I am good enough. I will look for all people who reflect my feelings of adequacy.

HOW DO THOUGHTS MAKE UP OUR WORLD?

Our reality is a reflection of our innermost thoughts and beliefs.

However, thoughts can become very powerful and influential. It is because our thoughts influence our emotions, and our feelings influence our actions.

Emotion science studies how emotions influence our thoughts, behaviours, and physiology.

One of the essential things that emotion science has taught us is that our emotions are not caused by events or circumstances in the external world. Instead, our emotions are created by our thoughts about those events or circumstances.

For example, let's say you get a flat tire on your way to work. You might feel frustrated, annoyed, or even angry. But it's not the flat tire itself that is causing these emotions. Instead, your thoughts about the flat tire are causing the feelings.

If you're thinking something like, "This is so annoying! I can't believe this is happening to me!" you will likely feel frustrated.

But if you're thinking something like, "This isn't a big deal. It's just a flat tire. It's not like it's the end of the world," then you'll likely feel much better.

How we think about ourselves and the world around us affects our physiology. Our bodies respond when stressed, anxious, or scared. We might feel our heart rate increase, our muscles tense up, or we might sweat.

Conversely, our physiology reflects that when we're feeling happy, relaxed, and safe. We might feel our heart rate slows down, our muscles relax, and we even start to smile.

The link between our thoughts, emotions, and physiology is so strong that it's impossible to separate them. They are all interconnected and influence each other.

So if we're feeling stressed, it's not because of our situation but our thoughts about it.

It's good news because it means we can change our emotions by changing our thoughts.

Author Mike George on stress: "The first place to look for the causes of stress is not out there; it's in here - in our heads."

It is why self-consciousness is so essential. When we are self-conscious, we can see our thoughts for what they are: electrical impulses in the brain.

We can see that our thoughts are not facts and do not define us.

How to become aware of what's going on inside your head?

Getting closer to what's going on in our minds is an exercise, which demands a lot of alertness and stillness, and it will become more accessible and more automatic with time.

Exercise

Start by observing your thoughts throughout the day. Notice when you're having negative thoughts, and try to pay attention to the content of your thoughts and the emotions they are accompanied by.

Then, once you've become more aware of your thoughts, start questioning them.

Ask yourself if the thoughts are true. Are they based on facts?

Are they helpful? Will dwelling on the thoughts make you feel better or worse?

If the answer is "worse," then it's time to let the thoughts go because it's pure fiction created by your mind. We will get back to this later in the book.

Five steps to understand your mind:

1. Pay attention to your emotions.
2. Identify the thoughts that are causing your emotions.
3. Question your thoughts. Are they true?
4. Choose which thoughts to believe and which to ignore.
5. Practice self-compassion.

Maybe you have noticed that when you are nervous about something, you tend to have an inner voice, saying things like "you're going to fail" or "you're not good enough".

These thoughts are called self-defeating thoughts and are usually based on irrational beliefs.

The first step in dealing with self-defeating thoughts is to become aware of them. Then, pay attention to when you're having these thoughts.

Another example is when you are angry with somebody, you can't stop telling him how stupid he is in your mind or how much you don't like him.

Then, once you've become more aware of your thoughts, start questioning them.

HOW DO THOUGHTS MAKE UP OUR WORLD?

Ask yourself if the thoughts are true. Are they based on facts? And how would you be in the situation without your belief?

These are called "negative spirals" because they cause us to feel worse and worse the longer we dwell on them.

The key to breaking out of a negative spiral is becoming aware of the thoughts causing your emotions. Then, once you've identified the thoughts, you can start questioning them.

If the answer is "no" to any of these questions, it's time to let the thoughts go.

The final step in dealing with self-defeating thoughts is to practice self-compassion.

Self-compassion is the ability to be kind and understanding to yourself, even when you make mistakes or have negative thoughts.

When self-compassionate, you don't beat yourself up for having negative thoughts.

Instead, you treat yourself with the kindness and understanding you would offer a friend. If you find self-compassionating challenging, imagine what you would say to a friend in the same situation.

Then, say those things to yourself.

How stressful feelings come about?

Stressful feelings emerge because we believe a thought we assume to be accurate.

This belief is usually based on irrational thoughts, such as "I can't handle this" or "I'm not good enough."

These thoughts create stress in our minds and bodies—the author, Mike George's thoughts on stress.

"The primary cause of stress is not the external situation but our thoughts about it."

"It's not events that trigger our reactions but rather our beliefs about them."

"If we believe that something is going to be difficult or painful, we will tend to experience stress. But if we believe we can handle the situation, we tend to feel calm and confident."

When we are stressed, our bodies go into "fight-or-flight" mode.

This survival mechanism is designed to help us deal with what the brain defines as energy-demanding situations.

HOW DO THOUGHTS MAKE UP OUR WORLD?

However, when this mechanism is triggered by stress, it can adversely affect our health. The fight-or-flight response causes our bodies to release stress hormones, such as adrenaline and cortisol.

These hormones increase our heart rate and blood pressure, and they can also suppress our immune system. Over time, chronic stress can lead to serious health problems like heart disease, high blood pressure, and depression.

The first step to dealing with stress is to become aware of your thoughts. Pay attention when you're having negative thoughts about a situation. Then, start to question the beliefs.

Are they true?

Why do we believe so strongly in thoughts that make us sick?

We often treat our thoughts as if they are gospel truths. We believe them without question and allow them to control our emotions and behaviour.

But why do we do this?

There are two main reasons:

1. We are unaware that we are doing it.
2. We believe our thoughts are a reality and define who we are.

The first reason is easy to understand. If we're unaware of the thoughts running through our minds, we can't question them.

We believe whatever we're thinking without realizing we're doing it.

The second reason is a little more complicated. It has to do with the way our brains are wired.

Our brains are designed to create thoughts that match our experiences and construct the best guess of reality.

However, these thoughts are only occasionally accurate. Moreover, they are often distorted and biased.

But because we believe our thoughts are a reality, we tend to react to them as if they are true. They can lead to a lot of stress and anxiety.

The good news is that we can learn to question our thoughts.

When we become aware of the thoughts causing us stress, we can examine them more closely.

Are they true? Do they make sense?

Are there other ways of looking at the situation?

By questioning our thoughts, we can see the situation more clearly.

And when we see things more clearly, we can respond to them more helpfully and productively.

HOW DO THOUGHTS MAKE UP OUR WORLD?

When we believe our thoughts are who we are, it can be tough to challenge them.

We may feel like we're not good enough or can't handle a situation.

These thoughts can lead to feelings of inadequacy and insecurity. And when we feel this way, it's hard to take action because we often believe our thoughts to be who we are. Without our story, who are we?

The first step is acknowledging that our thoughts are not who we are. We have thoughts. We are not our thoughts.

The only one who is responsible for your stress is you. Sometimes we blame society, our boss, spouse, kids or friends for how we feel. The truth is, we are the ones that allowed these thoughts to enter our minds in the first place.

No one can make us think or feel anything without our consent.

For far too long, we've all bought into the false belief that stress is a necessary evil. We've been told that to be successful, we must push ourselves to the brink of burnout and that any semblance of calm is a sign of weakness. It couldn't be further from the truth!

Not only is stress counterproductive, but it's also incredibly harmful to our mental and physical health.

So if you're ready to let go of the stress-inducing beliefs holding you back, keep reading.

Myth #1: Stress Is Necessary for Success
One of the most common myths about stress is that it's necessary to achieve success. We've all been told that to reach our goals; we must push ourselves to the brink of burnout. It couldn't be further from the truth.

Research has shown that stressed-out people are less productive than their calm and collected counterparts. So the next time you're overwhelmed by your to-do list, take a deep breath and remind yourself that peace of mind is key to getting things done.

Myth #2: Only Weak People Can't Handle Stress
We live in a society that values strength and productivity above all else. As a result, we've come to believe that only weak people can't handle stress. It couldn't be further from the truth! In reality, everyone experiences stress at some point in their lives.

How we deal with it determines whether or not it will overwhelm us. If you're struggling to cope with a stressful situation, reaching out for help is essential instead of trying to tough it out on your own. There's no shame in admitting that you need support!

Myth #3: Calm People are Lazy People
Another myth about stress is that calm people are lazy people. It couldn't be further from the truth! Just because someone can maintain inner peace doesn't mean they're not ambitious or driven.

Many of history's most successful people were also some of the most Zen. The next time you judge someone for being "too relaxed," remember that still waters run deep.

Myth #4: Stress Is an inevitable Part of Life
One of the most harmful myths about stress is that it's an inevitable part of life. We've all been told there's just no way to avoid it. But this isn't true! While it's true that some amount of stress is inevitable, there are plenty of things we can do to minimize its impact on our lives.

By making self-care a priority and learning how to manage our stressors, we can drastically reduce our overall stress levels.

Myth #5: Only Serious Things Deserve Our attention

The final myth about stress we're going bust is the belief that only serious things deserve our attention.

We often convince ourselves that relaxation and downtime are frivolous and unproductive. But this isn't true! On the contrary, taking time for yourself is one of the best things you can do for your mental health. When you allow yourself to relax and recharge, you'll be better able to deal with stressful situations when they arise.

If you're ready to achieve inner peace and release stress for good, start by busting these harmful myths! When you let go of these old paradigms, you make way for healthier relationships with yourself and those around you.

How emotions are formed

Lisa Feldman Barrett, a professor of psychology at Northeastern University and author of the book How Emotions are Made: The Secret Life of the Brain, explains that emotions are not just reactions to events that happen to us. Instead, they are constructs that our brains create based on our past experiences.

When we have a new experience, our brain will look for similar experiences from the past and try to match them up. Based on this information, it will then generate a feeling.

For example, if you've ever been embarrassed in front of a group of people, your brain will remember that experience and might create a feeling of shame the next time you're in a similar situation.

The brain is constantly trying to predict what will happen next based on what has happened in the past. Lisa Feldman Barrett says that the brain is always in the present, but it's always trying to anticipate what will happen next.

The brain makes emotions by considering three things:

1. Your body's current state,
2. Your past experiences
3. The situation you're in, your body's current state includes heart rate, breathing, and hormone levels.

Your past experiences include everything that has ever happened to you.

Your situation includes who else is around, what time it is, and what's happening. Based on all of this information, your brain will generate a feeling.

For example, if you're in a meeting and your boss criticizes you, your body might feel tense.

If you've had similar experiences in the past where you were criticized, your brain will try to match the current situation with those past experiences.

Based on this information it will generate a feeling. For example, the feeling might be anxiety, shame, or anger.

Just because our brain creates a feeling doesn't mean it is real.

How do we know?

The best way to know if our emotions are accurate is to pay attention to our body's physical reactions. Lisa Feldman Barrett says that our bodies are like a barometer for our feelings.

If we're feeling stressed, we might notice that our heart rate speeds up, we start to sweat, or we feel tense. These physical reactions can be a good indicator of whether or not our emotions are accurate.

Sometimes, we might have an emotional reaction that doesn't match the situation. For example, you might feel embarrassed even though no one is laughing at you. In this case, your brain might create the feeling based on an experience you once had and forgot all about.

The good news is that we can change how our brain creates emotions.

Lisa Feldman Barrett says that the key to freedom is self-consciousness. When we become aware of the thoughts causing our stress, we can start questioning them. But does this mean that we can not blame others for our stress?

Yes, it does. Lisa Feldman Barrett says that we are the ones in control of our thoughts and feelings. Therefore, no one can make us feel anything without our consent.

Mihaly Csikszentmihalyi was a Hungarian psychologist who researched happiness and well-being extensively.

He says there are two types of emotions: basic and complex.

Primary emotions are the emotions that we feel in response to events that happen to us. These emotions are universal, meaning that everyone experiences them.

Examples of basic emotions include happiness, sadness, anger, fear, and love.

Complex emotions are the ones we create based on our thoughts and beliefs. These emotions are unique to each individual.

Examples of complex emotions include anxiety, shame, and jealousy.

Csikszentmihalyi says that we have more control over our complex emotions than our basic emotions.

It is because our thoughts create complex emotions, and we can choose what thoughts to focus on.

For example, if we're feeling anxious about a presentation we have to give, we can choose to focus on thoughts that will make us feel more confident.

Or, if we're feeling jealous of our friend's success, we can focus on supportive and happy thoughts for them.

HOW DO THOUGHTS MAKE UP OUR WORLD?

We create our emotions by the way we think about our experiences. And we can change how we think, which means we can change how we feel.

Our thoughts and feelings are often based on assumptions and predictions, rather than reality. And these predictions are often inaccurate.

How we interpret a situation determines how we feel about it.

For example, if you're waiting in line at the grocery store and the person in front of you is taking a long time, you might think, "This is so annoying. I'm never going to get out of here."

This thought would likely create the emotion of anger.

But if you thought, "I'm glad I have this extra time to relax," you would likely feel calmer and more relaxed.

As you can see, it's not the situation that determines how we feel. It's our thoughts about the situation.

It means that we have a lot of control over our emotions. We can choose how we want to feel by choosing our thoughts about a specific situation.

CHAPTER 3
Reality is kinder than we think

The author Byron Katie says that reality is what is happening right now. Reality is what we see, hear, smell, taste, and ouch. It's the present moment. Anil Seth, a neuroscientist, says that reality is what we make of the present moment. He says that our brains always make predictions about what will happen next.

We suffer when we fight against reality and try to control what's happening.

For example, you're suffering if you're stuck in traffic and angry about it. However, if you accept that you're stuck in traffic and find a way to make the best of it, you're not suffering.

When we try to control reality, we try to control the impossible. We can't control other people's actions, the weather, or the economy. The only thing we can control is our thoughts and actions.

One way to stop fighting reality is to become more aware of our thoughts and the stories we tell ourselves about reality.

Reality is what is without our story.

Another example is that you have been invited for a job interview, and you are afraid they will discover that you don't know anything, regardless of more than 20 years of experience in the field.

The reality is that you have been invited for a job interview. But, unfortunately, the story you're telling yourself is that you will fail.

The reality is neutral. Our thoughts and stories about reality create our emotions, making us believe that what we experience is the truth. So, which prediction is reality? The answer is both. One is just kinder than another.

Our brains constantly make predictions, but we are still determining what will happen. So all we can do is trust that reality will be kinder than our thoughts about reality.

We don't see reality as it is because we're constantly filtering reality through our thoughts, emotions, and past experiences.

How we interpret a situation determines how we feel about it. So it's not reality that scares me; it's my thoughts about reality.

For example, if you're walking down the street and you see a dog coming towards you, you might think, "That dog is going to attack me." This thought would likely create the emotion of fear.

But if you thought, "That dog is so cute! I hope it comes over to say hi," you would likely feel happier and more excited.

As you can see, the reality is neutral. It's our thoughts about the reality that create our emotions.

Maybe you think, what about wars, pandemics, people getting laid off, people dying? How can that be kind?

The reality is that those things are happening, but our thoughts about them create our emotions.

For example, if you're thinking about a pandemic, you might think, "I'm so scared. I'm going to die." This thought would likely create the emotion of fear.

But if you thought, "I'm grateful that I have a roof over my head and food to eat in a difficult situation," you would likely feel calmer and more grateful and capable of helping people who need your help in a concrete situation.

It's not reality that is scary; it's our thoughts about reality.

The distinction between reality and fiction

It's often blurred because we tend to believe our thoughts about reality.

For example, you might think, "I'm not good enough." This is just a thought; it's not reality. But if you believe this thought, it will feel like reality.

The reality is that you are just as worthy and deserving as anyone else, but the thought "I'm not good enough" creates the emotion of insecurity and unworthiness.

Thoughts are just thoughts; they're not real. But if we believe them, they become our reality.

That is why it's essential to become aware of our thoughts and the stories we tell ourselves about reality. When we become aware of our thoughts, we can question them and see if they're true.

For example, let's say you have the thought, "I'm not good enough."

You might question this thought by asking yourself, "Is this true? How do I know this is true? What evidence do I have that this is true?"

When you question your thoughts, you see they're just thoughts; they're not real. And when you know that they're just thoughts, you can start to let them go.

And then let the thought go. Reality is what is without our story.

Why do we tell ourselves fake stories about reality? We tell ourselves stories about reality because it makes us believe we can control reality.

If we believe that reality is what we think it is, then we can control our thoughts and make reality the way we want it to be.

But the reality is what it is; we can't control it. And trying to control reality only leads to suffering.

The only thing we can control is our thoughts about reality. And when we become aware of our thoughts, we can start questioning them and seeing if they're true.

So the next time you find yourself caught up in a story about reality not feeling good, take a step back and ask yourself, "Is this true? How do I know this is true? What evidence do I have that this is?

It's a way to cope with the uncertainty of life.

For example, let's say you're worried about getting laid off.

You might tell yourself the story that you're going to get laid off, and then you'll never be able to find another job, and you'll end up homeless and penniless.

This story might make you feel better in the short term because it's a way to cope with the uncertainty of not knowing what will happen.

But this story will only make you feel worse long-term because it's not reality.

The reality is that you don't know what's going to happen, and worrying about it doesn't change anything.

Only you are responsible for your happiness

What is happiness?
Happiness is a state of mind. It's not something that you can find outside of yourself.

You might need things to be happy, like a successful career, a big house, or money.

But these things won't necessarily make you happy. On the contrary, they might even make you unhappy.

The only person who is responsible for your happiness is you.

You are the only one who can control your thoughts and emotions. So to be happy, you must start with your thoughts and feelings.

No one outside of yourself can ever give you what you want.

So the next time you find yourself waiting for someone or something to make you happy, remember that only you can do that.

The best teachers constantly surround us. The people who surround you every day are the best teachers. Your family, friends, co-workers, and even strangers can teach you something if you're open to learning.

You might not realize it, but everyone around you is teaching you something.

For example, your co-worker might be teaching you how to be patient.

Your friend might be teaching you how to be a good listener.

And the stranger on the bus might be teaching you how to be kind.

So the next time you find yourself surrounded by people who get on your nerves, remember that they're all teaching you something.

Ten things to be aware of to invite more happiness into your life:

1. Accept reality as it is, not as you want it to be.
2. Give up the past.
3. Be present in the moment.
4. Don't take things personally.
5. Don't make assumptions.
6. Communicate clearly.
7. Be grateful for what you have.
8. Let go of attachment to outcomes.
9. Surrender to what is.
10. Trust the process of life.

We can't control what happens to us, but we can control how we react.

So if you want to invite more happiness into your life, start by accepting reality as it is, not as you want it to be. Then let go of the past and be present in the moment.

And finally, don't take things personally. Communicate, be grateful for what you have, and let go of attachment to outcomes. Trust that the process of life will unfold exactly as it's supposed to.

Einstein on happiness:

"The most important thing is to enjoy your life—to be happy—it's all that matters."

REALITY IS KINDER THAN WE THINK

"There are only two ways to live your life. One is as though nothing is a miracle. The other is as though everything is a miracle."

"The pursuit of happiness is a meaningless goal because happiness is not something you can pursue. It's something you have to find within yourself."

If you want to be happy, stop chasing after things you think will make you happy.

Instead, look within yourself and find the source of happiness.

And remember, as Einstein said, "everything is a miracle." So appreciate all the miracles in your life, big and small. That's what will make you truly happy.

CHAPTER 4

When you give, you receive

It's been scientifically proven that grateful people are happier people. So if you want to be happy, start by being thankful for what you have.

Gratitude has several benefits.

It can improve your physical health, mental health, and overall well-being.

It can also increase your resilience in the face of stress, help you recover from trauma more quickly, and make you more likely to help others.

So if you want to be happy and healthy, start by practicing gratitude.

You can do this by keeping a gratitude journal, where you write down things you're grateful for each day. Or you can take a few moments each day to reflect on what you're grateful for and why.

The key is to focus on the positive aspects of your life, no matter how small they may be.

THE TIPPING POINT

When you start practicing gratitude, you'll find that your whole outlook on life will change. You'll be happier, healthier, and more resilient. And you'll be amazed at how much goodness is all around you.

When you're grateful, you feel a sense of abundance. You feel like there's more than enough to go around.

You also feel connected to other people and to the world around you.

And finally, gratefulness creates a sense of well-being.

So the next time you feel unhappy, take a moment to appreciate all the good things in your life. Start with the simple things, like the air you breathe and the food you eat.

Then move on to the people in your life who you appreciate.

And finally, think about all the accomplishments and blessings you've received.

You'll find happiness when you take the time to appreciate all you have.

Allow yourself to savor the feeling of happiness and gratitude. And when you do, you'll find that your life is infinitely more abundant than you ever realized.

So if you want to invite more happiness into your life, start by practicing gratitude.

Benefits of gratitude:

1. Gratitude helps us appreciate what we have instead of constantly chasing after things we think will make us happy.
2. Gratitude makes us happier and more optimistic.
3. Gratitude reduces our negative emotions and makes us less likely to experience depression.

Think about all the good things in your life, big and small.

Be thankful for your health, family and friends, job, home, and everything else that makes up your life.

The more grateful you are, the happier you'll be. And the happier you are, the more likely you will attract even more good things into your life.

The only time you receive is when you give. So if you want to be happy, make it your goal to help others.

You can start by volunteering your time for a worthy cause. Or you can donate money to a charity that you care about.

You can also act with kindness and compassion in your everyday life.

Every time you give, you open yourself up to receiving even more.

And the more you receive, the more you'll have to give. So it's a beautiful cycle of giving and receiving that will bring more happiness into your life and the world around you.

The reality is that we are all just looking for love. We want to be loved and accepted for who we are.

And when we don't feel loved, we go out into the world looking for it.

But the ironic thing is that the more we chase after love, the more elusive it becomes.

Only when we stop chasing after love and start giving it unconditionally can we find true happiness.

Unconditional love is one of the most potent forces in the universe. It can heal wounds, transform lives, and bring hope where there was none.

When you give love unconditionally, you open yourself up to receiving it in return.

And when you receive love, it fills you up and overflows into the lives of those around you.

So if you want to be happy, make it your mission to spread love wherever you go.

Be kind to strangers, forgive those who have wronged you, and show compassion for those suffering.

And most importantly, always remember to love yourself. When you do, you'll find that happiness is never far away.

Let go of any attachments

It's an illusion that we own anything; we manage something in a period until it's time to let go.

Everything is in constant change and flow, and so is our life.

Eckhart Tolle says: "Attachment is the great fabricator of illusions; reality can only be attained by someone who is detached."

So if you want to be happy, learn to let go of your attachments. Let go of your attachment to material possessions, other people, and your ego.

How do I recognise when my ego is the CEO in my life?

- You need to be right all the time.
- You're always looking for validation from others.
- You have a hard time admitting when you're wrong.
- You find it difficult to let go of grudges and resentments.
- You're constantly comparing yourself to others.
- You have a fear of failure.
- You're never satisfied with what you have.

The reality is that the ego is an illusion. It's not who we are. When we let go of our attachment to the ego, we open ourselves up to true happiness.

Imagine your ego being your confused teenager, and you treat him with love and indulgence every time he passes.

He is just a part of you that will grow out of it, given some time and space.

So if you want to be happy, learn to love your ego instead of being controlled by it.

Have you noticed that It's not the object you're attached to; it's the meaning you've assigned to that object?

For example, you might be attached to your car because it represents your success and status.

Or you might be attached to your house because it symbolizes your security, where your kids have been brought up.

It's not the object you're attached to; it's the story behind it. The only thing you lose when you let go of your belongings is a story.

What are we afraid of? Byron Katie has this answer; to lose what we have and not get what we want.

So if we have attachment issues, it's because we're afraid of not getting what we want or losing what we have.

The reality is that nothing is permanent. Everything is always in a state of change.

So if you want to be happy, learn to let go of your attachment to things, people, and outcomes.

Focus on the present moment.

Eckhart Tolle says: "The past gives you an identity, and the future holds the promise of salvation, of fulfilment in what presently eludes you."

So if you want to be happy, focus on the present moment. Don't dwell on the past or worry about the future. Just be here now.

The reality is that the present moment is all we have. It's all there is.

Tell me how you treat others, and I will tell you who you are

Growing up, we have been told stories founded on thoughts by parents, teachers, and society. Stories we believe to be accurate, which they are not. All stories are fake because they are stories.

Yuval Noah Harari describes it: "Fiction has become more powerful than reality because fiction is often more effective than reality in shaping human emotions and behaviour."

Our stories are who we believe us to be because they are given to us very early before cognition and emotions are developed enough for us to question them. And we hold on to these stories because they give us a sense of identity and because it is difficult to let go of something that has been such an integral part of our lives for so long.

If we believe our stories define who we are, how can we question them if we don't consider them an appendix?

An excellent starting point is recognising that these stories are not reality. Instead, they are thoughts we have been told and believe to be true.

From there, we can begin to question our stories. Why do we believe them? Are they serving us?

It can be a difficult and painful process, but it is so worth it when we finally let go of the stories holding us back and preventing us from living our best lives.

> "The greatest enemy of a better future is often the nostalgia for a better past."
>
> - *Yuval Noah Harari*

To be happy, we must let go of the nostalgia for a better past and focus on creating a better future.

How we treat others reflects how we see and feel about ourselves often. We seldom meet the other where she is but where we are. Byron Katie formulated it like this:

"I am not upset for a reason. I am upset because my thoughts are making me upset."

An example of this is anger. You are not angry at the other person; you are mad because your thoughts about the situation make you mad.

More examples:
- If you feel insecure, your thoughts make you feel insecure.
- If you feel unloved, your thoughts are making you feel unloved.
- If you feel anxious, your thoughts make you anxious.

The reality is that our thoughts create our reality. When we are busy judging our neighbour, saying he should do this or that, the reality is that we are judging ourselves. When we get still and have an open mind, we see that what we want others to do, we need to do ourselves.

- You can only be loyal to others if you are loyal to yourself.
- You can only give what you have. If you want to give love, love yourself first.

- If you want to give compassion, be compassionate to yourself first.
- If you want to give forgiveness, forgive yourself first.

The reality is that we can only give others what we have within us. So if you want to be happy, start by giving yourself what you want from others.

Why are there so many angry people in the world?

The reality is that people are angry because their thoughts are making them angry. If they could only see that their thoughts cause their anger, they could let go of it and be at peace.

Why do we become angry?

We become angry when we believe that reality should be different.

When we are attached to the way things should be, we suffer. We need to learn to let go of our attachment to the way things should be and accept reality for what it is.

So often, we are our own worst enemies when it comes to love. We get in our way by believing that reality should be different. If we could only let go of these beliefs, we would be free to love fully and unconditionally.

> "Resentment is like drinking poison and hoping it will kill your enemies."
> - *Nelson Mandela*

The reality is that resentment does nothing but hurt us. It doesn't hurt the person we resent; it only hurts us. If we could see that, we could let go of our resentment and focus on more.

We get angry because we think reality should be different than it is. We believe people should behave differently; the world should be different. The truth is that things are the way they are. People are the way they are. And we can't change them.

The only thing we can change is how we think about the world, and then the world changes.

- If we want more love in the world, we need to be more loving.

- If we want more compassion, we need to be more compassionate.
- If we want more understanding, we need to be more understanding.
- If we want more peace, we need to be more peaceful.

Dr. Dicken Bettinger says that the only way to change the world is to change ourselves. So if you want to be happy, focus on changing yourself and watch as the world around you changes too.

CHAPTER 5

Everything is Okay

Nothing comes from nothing is an old saying that is still used today. It means that everything has a cause and happens for a reason. Is this true?

We live in a world we believe we control and understand, but the reality is that we don't.

The reality is that we don't know what's going to happen tomorrow. We don't know what's going to happen in the next minute. We can make plans and hope for the best, but we can't know what will happen.

It can be a scary thought, but it doesn't have to be. Why not?

Because the reality is that we don't have to know, we can't know. And that's okay.

What does this mean for us? It means that we need to be okay with not knowing. We need to be okay with the uncertainty of life.

It doesn't mean that we should sit back and do nothing. It just means we should trust that everything will work out.

When we live in the reality of not knowing, we are free. We are free to be ourselves, and we are free to make our own choices.

We don't have to worry about what other people think or what they want us to do. Instead, we can focus on being our best selves and doing what we believe is right.

The don't know mind and leadership

In leadership positions, living in the reality of not knowing is imperative. Does this surprise you?

It shouldn't.

Leaders are often expected to have all the answers. But the reality is that they don't. They can't.

The best leaders are those who are comfortable with not knowing. They are fine with the uncertainty of life.

They question their beliefs and are curious about what they don't know they don't know. They are constantly learning and growing.

The best leaders also realise that they can't control everything. They know that some things are out of their hands. And they are okay with that. They focus on what they can control and let go of the rest.

When we are in leadership positions, we must remember that we can have some of the answers. However, we must be okay with not knowing and believe everything will work out.

Most people would claim it's essential for leaders who know and are not insecure.

The reality is that the only thing we can do as leaders is to make the best decision we can at the moment and then have faith that it will all work out in the end.

It doesn't mean we should be reckless or careless with our decisions. However, we must be okay with not knowing and believing everything will work out.

So the next time you find yourself in a leadership position, remember that it's okay not to know. It's okay to be uncertain. And it's okay to have faith that everything will work out in the end. Reality check!

When we live in the reality of not knowing, we are free to be ourselves and focus on what's truly important.

Have faith that you are doing the best you can and that everything will work out in the end. Everything always does.

To be present

Try this little exercise; for the next five minutes in complete quiet, you will follow your thoughts. Pay attention to how much time is spent in the past or future.

Your thoughts seldom have anything to do with reality as it is right now in the given moment.

It is what most people do. They pay attention to judging everything that comes to mind.

"He is too big", "That dress is too red".

Now you try to observe without adding any value to what you notice; for example, you look at a flower, person, or car without giving it a score.

You see a car, and almost immediately, you tell yourselves: Oh, That's a car. And then you start adding to the description of the old red Volvo even though your brain had concluded it was an older-style red Volvo long ago. It seems like the brain tells you what you already know to reassure you that you are in charge even though you are not.

You just see it for what it is.

This little exercise will train you to be present in the moment. Your mind will be where your body is instead of running into the past or future all the time. The more you train to be present, the easier it will get, and reality will look very different.

Time expands when we learn to be more aware of existing in the present moment because life becomes more prosperous.

It is said that when we die, our life will pass before our eyes in a fraction of a second. This exercise is a way of training to live our life more fully so that we don't regret anything when it's time to leave this reality because we have been present in each step.

How come we find it so difficult or scary to be in the present moment when reality is only here and now?

The answer to this might be that we have been taught that reality is something different.

We have been taught that reality is what we see on TV, in the news or read about in the paper.

But the reality is not what we see on a screen. The truth is not what we read about in the news. Reality is what's happening right here, right now. Reality is the flowers blooming outside, the birds singing, and the sun shining. Reality is our breathing in and out, our heart beating and our thoughts passing by.

The music unfolds in the silence between the notes. The space between our thoughts in the present moment creates a pure being.

Meet your teacher

The teacher you are looking for is already within you. All the answers to your questions are inside of you. So you must learn to listen to your inner voice and intuition.

Your intuition is that little voice inside you that knows what's best for you. That little voice is always trying to guide you in the right direction.

A good teacher is also a good student. It means that you need to be willing to learn. You need to be open to new ideas and ways of doing things. You also need to be patient with yourself. Learning how to listen to your intuition takes time and practice.

Michael A. Singer, the author of "The Untethered Soul", says that you are the teacher you've been looking for your whole life.

"The teacher you seek is not outside you, but within you. The answers to your questions are also within you. The only thing preventing you from finding these answers is your mind."

Singer says that "the key to freedom is to realize that you are not your mind."

In other words, you are not your thoughts. Yet, you are the one who is observing your thoughts.

You are the witness to your own life. How do you know this?

The answer is simple. A feeling follows every thought you have.

- If you are thinking about something that happened in the past, you will feel nostalgia or regret.
- If you are thinking about something that might happen in the future, you will feel fear or anxiety.

If you are present in the moment and not thinking about the past or the future, you will feel peace and calm, so the key to freedom is learning to be present at the moment.

The common misconception is that you must understand the past to see the future. It is not valid. You do not need to understand the past to see the future. You only need to be present at the moment. When you are present in the moment, you can see things. Your past experiences do not influence you. You are simply observing what is happening right now.

We don't do it often because we fear the present moment. We are afraid of what we might see if we are truly present.

We might see that we are not who we think we are. We might see that our life is going differently than we want it to. We might not be as happy as we want.

However, it is only by being present in the moment that we can truly see reality for what it is and make the necessary changes to create the life we want.

So, if you're ready to meet your teacher, start by learning to be present. Observe your thoughts and feelings without judgment.

How will being present influence your everyday life? Well, for starters, you will be less reactive to the things around you:

- You will no longer be a victim of your circumstances. You can see what is happening and make the best choices for you.
- You will also be more mindful of your thoughts and actions.
- Your decision become better. When you are truly present, your intuition will guide you to make the best decision for yourself.
- You will be more creative. When you are not thinking about the past or the future, your mind can be creative and develop new ideas.
- You will have better relationships. You can listen to others and be fully present in the conversation when you are present. It creates a deeper connection with the other person.
- You will feel more peaceful and calm. When you are not worrying about the future or dwelling on the past, you can live in the present moment and find peace and calmness.
- You will be able to achieve better things because you will be more explicit about what you want.

- Your mind will not be full of doubts, so you can focus on what is essential to achieving your goal. As a result, you will have more energy to pursue your dreams.
- You will enjoy the process and the journey, not just the destination. Because in the present moment, there is only the journey.
- Your productivity will improve. When you are truly present, your mind is clear and focused. As a result, you can better utilize your time and energy to achieve your goals.
- You will find it easier to stick to your goals because you will be more aware of your thoughts and actions. As a result, you will be less likely to make excuses or allow yourself to be distracted from your goals.
- You will find it easier to live in the moment and enjoy life. Why? Because you will have less clutter in your mind. You can focus on what is happening right now and enjoy the moment.
- Your motivation will come from within, not from external factors. When you are motivated by something external, it is easy to lose motivation when things get tough. However, when your push comes from within, you will

likely stick to your goals even when things get tough.

The goal is not to control your thoughts or eliminate them. Instead, the goal is to become aware of them.

When do you know to change?

You will know when to change when you feel like you're holding on to something tight and it's causing you pain. Likewise, you will know when to change when you feel like you're struggling and fighting against reality.

Byron Katie is an American speaker and author who teaches a method of self-inquiry known as "The Work," which helps you gain clarity on your thoughts and reality.

The Work consists of four questions you can ask yourself about any stressful thought:

1. Is it true?
2. Can you know that it's true?
3. How do you react? What happens when you believe that thought?
4. Who would you be without the thought?

Answer these four questions for each of your negative thoughts and see what changes.

The goal is not to believe or disbelieve your thoughts. The goal is to question them.

You can start by asking yourself, "Is this thought true?"

If the answer is yes, ask yourself, "Can I know it's true?"

If the answer is no, ask yourself, "What would I be like without this thought?"

The third step is to turn your thoughts around.

The goal is not to believe the opposite of your thought. Instead, the goal is to find a way to see the situation from another perspective.

For example, if your thought is "I'm not good enough," you can turn it around to "I'm good enough."

Or, if your thought is, "People are always trying to control me," you can turn it around to "I'm always trying to control people."

The fourth step is to find evidence for your new thought.

The goal is not to believe your new thought. The goal is to find evidence that supports it.

For example, if your new thought is "I'm good enough," you can look for evidence of times when you have been good enough.

Or, if your new thought is, "I'm always trying to control people," you can look for evidence of times when you have been controlling.

The goal is not to eliminate negative thoughts or force yourself to believe positive ones. Instead, the goal is simply to become aware of your thoughts and reality. And by doing so, you will find more peace and calmness.

It will change how you meet your boss, peers, spouse, kids, and reality.

It will also change how reality meets you. The moment you let go of the thought; My boss doesn't like me, you meet her in the cantine. And the truth is; that she wants to ask you for help with a project.

You will listen with new ears, see with fresh eyes, and feel with a new heart.

And reality will become more magical than you ever thought possible.

CHAPTER 6

No one can hurt me but me

Well, if you are attached to how things should be, that's my business. If you're bound to how things should be, that's your business. And we can both see that we're never going to get what we want that way.

So my business is not to try to control your reality, and your business is not to try to hold mine. My reality is just fine, and so is yours.

I'm concerned with what is not my business when judging reality, trying to control reality, or making reality into a problem.

Though I would consider a pandemic a problem and not forget a war like the one in the Ukraine. If I accept reality like a war, it feels like I approve of it, but I don't.

I can grieve for the reality and do something about it. That's what makes reality my business:

What can I do? When we're clear that our only business is reality—What is?—we see that what is happening has nothing to do with us. And we're free to act.

Without my story, there shouldn't be a war in the Ukraine; what can I do?

- Fundraise
- Create awareness
- Help with what is needed
- Write a letter to the people who are in power

Reality is what is happening, not my story about what is happening. I can do something about it when I have a clear mind.

The problem is that my story is almost always based on judgments, and judgments create separation. When I judge reality, I do not see reality as it is. I see reality through my own opinion, my point of view.

And when I am attached to my point of view, I am not open to reality. I am not available to what is happening. I am not open to the possibility that there may be another way to see the situation.

So, when I'm busy with something which is none of my business, instead of dealing with my own business, problems keep on existing and growing more significant.

We're not open to reality when we're caught up in our opinions. And when we're not open to the fact, we cannot see the truth. We're not able to see what is happening.

The truth is that reality is constantly changing. And that's why reality is our business: What can we learn from it? How can we be better prepared for it?

So, when we're clear and present and not attached to our opinion, reality can show us the way.

We're no longer attached to the outcome when we let go of our opinion. We're no longer attached to the way things should be. And when we're not attached to the way things should be, we're free to see reality as it is. And we're free to find our way forward.

The oxymorons of life

We often do it without paying attention; We use words that contradict each other and our actions.

We claim to want one thing, and then we go out and do something that completely contradicts what we say we want.

- When you say one thing and do the opposite, and not being aware of it.
- When you blame others for the behavior, you have.
- When you hold on to a belief you know is not valid.

It's essential to pay attention to the words you use because they create your reality. So, if you're not careful with your words, you can create a reality you don't want.

Words have power. And when we use words that contradict each other, we create confusion and chaos in our lives; some examples are:

- I can't do it.
- I don't have time.
- I'm not good enough.
- This is too hard.

These are all examples of words that contradict each other.

When you say, "I can't do it", you're saying that you're not capable of doing it. But then, when you say, "I don't have time", you're saying that you do have the time, but you're just choosing not to use it.

And when you say, "I'm not good enough", you're saying that you are good enough, but you don't believe it.

All of these contradictions create confusion and chaos in our lives. And when we're confused and cluttered, we cannot see reality.

We always have the time, are always good enough, and can always do it.

When we let go of the words contradicting each other, we can see reality more clearly. And when we know the truth, we're free to find our way forward.

In his book "Sapiens", Yuval Noah Harari talks about life's oxymorons.

Yuval Noah Harari talks about the war in Ukraine as an excellent example of an oxymoron.

"The Russian government wants to protect ethnic Russians in Ukraine. But the reality is that there are very few ethnic Russians living in Ukraine.

Most of the people who live in Ukraine are Ukrainians. And most of the people who are fighting in the war are Ukrainians. So, the reality is that the Russian government is not protecting ethnic Russians in Ukraine.

They use the pretext of protecting ethnic Russians to justify their political goals.

If we're not careful with our words, we can create a reality we don't want.

To sum it up.

We can see reality more clearly when we pay attention to the words we use. Then, we can see the truth.

Giving is receiving

When you give, you receive. It's a simple law of nature.

But for some reason, many of us have a hard time believing it. If we give, we'll end up with less.

The reality is that when you give, you receive. It's a law of nature. So when you give, you activate the law of reciprocity.

The law of reciprocity is a psychological phenomenon that occurs when we feel obliged to repay someone who has helped us.

Robert Cialdini, professor of psychology and marketing at Arizona State University, explains the law of reciprocity as "we feel the need to give back when we receive" because we want to maintain the balance in our relationships.

The law of reciprocity is one of the six principles of persuasion that Robert Cialdini talks about in his book "Influence: The Psychology of Persuasion".

He says that the law of reciprocity is one of the most powerful and effective persuasion techniques because it's based on our natural human tendency to want to repay someone who has helped us.

Reciprocity works in different situations; Businesses use it, charities use it, and even governments use it.

For example, let's say you're a business owner and give a customer a gift. The customer will feel obliged to repay you by buying something from you. Or, let's say you donate to a charity. The charity will feel obliged to refund you for doing good work. And in politics, when a politician helps, the person they help will feel obliged to repay them by voting for them.

The law of reciprocity is a strong tool for good or evil. It's up to us to decide how we want to use it. It's essential to be aware of it, so we can use it to benefit the people around us and us.

The law of reciprocity is compelling because it's hardwired into our psychology. It's something that we can't ignore.

- When you have invited friends over for dinner, they will say next time, we will cook for you.
- When you help a colleague with a project, they will return the favour.
- If you compliment someone, they will likely give you one in return.

Parker J. Palmer is an American writer, educator, and founder of the Center for Courage & Renewal. He has written extensively about education, community and leadership.

In his book "The Heart of Higher Education", he talks about how the law of reciprocity is at the heart of all human relationships.

He says that when we give, we open up the possibility of receiving. And when we receive, we open up the possibility of giving.

Giving and receiving are two sides of the same coin. They're two parts of the same whole.

And when we understand that, we can start creating relationships based on mutuality and reciprocity.

What is success for you?

Most people understand the importance of setting goals to achieve success. However, I am more interested in what success is.

Goals are most beneficial for the direction and motivation they give you. The value of goals is more emotional than tangible.

Therefore, pursuing your goals is more important than the goal itself.

> " When I look around, I see people pursuing goals by damaging their social life and reputation. Did they accomplish anything? I don't think so!"
>
> METTE REEBIRK

Research tells us that success is only sometimes about reaching the goals we set for ourselves. Instead, success comes from simply doing our best and enjoying the journey.

According to a study published in the Journal of Positive Psychology, people who focus on the process rather than the outcome are more likely to feel successful.

The study participants were asked to rate their success in various areas, such as their careers, relationships, and personal goals. They were also asked to report how much they enjoyed the process of pursuing these goals.

Again, the results showed that those who appreciated the process were more likely to feel successful, regardless of whether they achieved their goals.

So what does this mean for us?

First, it's important to remember that success is more than reaching a specific goal. It's also about enjoying the journey along the way.

If you can find ways to enjoy your work and life experiences, you're likely to feel successful no matter what happens.

For Yuval Noah Harari, an Israeli historian and bestselling author, success is not a destination. It's a journey. It's our choices, decisions and actions along the way.

In an interview with Big Think, he talked about the concept of success and how we should think about it. He said that if we want to be successful, we need to think about what we're doing today and how it will impact our tomorrow.

He pointed out that success is about more than achieving a specific goal. It's about the journey. It's about the choices we make and the actions we take along the way.

Harari's view of success has important implications for leadership.

To be successful leaders, we must focus on the journey, not the destination. We need to focus on the choices we make and the actions we take today, not on some future goal.

Goals that will change over time because the world changes in an uncontrolled manner.

It doesn't mean that goals are unimportant. Goals are still important. But they're not the most important thing.

More and more businesses realize that they are responsible for positively impacting society and that it starts with what we do today because it will influence tomorrow.

The way we think about success is changing. And it's changing because we realize that the old way of thinking is no longer sufficient.

We need to start thinking about success in a new way, one that takes into account the journey, not just the destination and KPIs.

People and, for that matter, businesses struggling to find their purpose and to believe that success should look a certain way, can relax:

- Your career can be something other than a straight line - it can be and often is zigzaggy.

- You can change direction - only a few do it.
- You can go back and forth - without feeling you go back to a dud.
- You can take detours. - without feeling, you are not professional.
- You can meander. - go with your flow.

And it's OK as long as you feel good about the steps you take, and if you recognise a stressful emotion, you know you need to examine whether what you believe about the now is the truth.

This shift has important implications for leadership. If we want to be successful leaders, we need to focus on making a positive impact, not just on making money. We need to think about how our choices and actions today impact tomorrow.

One business leader who works from this mindset is Bill Gates. Gates is, as we all know, the co-founder of Microsoft and one of the wealthiest men in the world. Bill Gates' definition of the concept of 'success' is:

"For me, success is not about me. It's about the impact I can have on the world."

This mindset has helped Gates achieve great things. But it's also helped him enjoy the journey.

"I love what I'm doing," he said. "I don't think there's anything else I'd rather be doing."

What are some implications of this mindset for leadership?

It is a powerful mindset for leaders. It's a mindset that says, when we think like this, we're more likely to make choices that align with our values and will positively impact the world.

Gandhi was an Indian political leader who fought for India's independence from British rule. He is also one of the most influential figures in world history.

Gandhi believed that every moment is essential and that every action we take has the potential to make a difference.

"There is no such thing as an insignificant act," he said. "Every act matters, and every person counts."

This philosophy guided Gandhi in all aspects of his life and work. And it's a philosophy that can guide us as well.

How can every one of us become successful regardless of what we are doing with the mindset that what I make today impacts tomorrow?

It starts by understanding that success is not about achieving a specific goal. It's about the journey. It's about the choices we make and the actions we take along the way. Some examples could be:

- Success is not about getting your students good grades if you're a teacher. It's about helping them learn and grow.
- If you're a doctor, success is about more than curing all of your patients. Instead, it's about helping them to heal and feel better so they can heal themselves.
- If you're a business owner, success is not about making money. It's about providing value for your customers and positively impacting society.
- If you are a leader, success is not about achieving specific goals. Instead, it's about positively impacting the people you lead and the world around you, by doing this, you will reach whatever floats your boat.

The old definition of success is no longer sufficient. Instead, we need to start thinking about success in a new way, one that considers the journey, not just the destination. When we do this, we open up new possibilities for ourselves and the world.

Exercise

Here are five questions to ponder over:

1. What is success for you in this new perspective?
2. How do you know when you've achieved it?
3. Is it something that can be measured or quantified?
4. Is it always relative to someone else's opinion or perspective?
5. If you don't believe in the concept of success, can you still achieve things others might deem as such?

What matters is the journey, not the destination. So focus on making choices that are in line with your values and that will have a positive impact on the world.

That's how you'll find authentic success and good grades; fewer sick people and more businesses and employees loving what they do will emerge naturally.

CHAPTER 7
How to get rid of stress?

It may be a surprise to learn that we are responsible for our stress. That's right - the majority of the stress that we experience is self-induced. And even more surprising is that we can learn to control it.

In this chapter, we'll explore some of the common myths about stress and identify some concrete steps that you can take to reduce the amount of stress in your life. So let's get started by busting some of those pesky myths!

Stress is a growing kind of pandemic in our society. The silent killer can lead to health problems, from anxiety and depression to heart disease and stroke.

More and more people understand that they have to change something. Companies likewise get it, because it costs them a lot of money in terms of health care and lost productivity.

What do we think about stress?

A really good question is: How are you feeling right now? If the answer is "stressed", "anxious", or "overwhelmed", it's time for a change.

There are many things you can do to reduce stress in your life. Exercise, eating healthy foods, getting enough sleep and spending time with positive people are great options.

You can do one more thing that will make a BIG difference. And that's to change the way you think about stress. Here are some common beliefs:

- Stress is suitable for you; it can help you achieve.
- Stress is a normal part of life, and a little rest will help you soon get you back in business.
- There's nothing you can do about stress; you have to deal with it.
- You have to be strong and push through tough times.

These are all myths!
Stress is not suitable for you, even a little bit. It's

not normal, and there's a lot you can do to reduce it. Let's explore these ideas in more depth.

When stressed, our bodies release cortisol, which helps us deal with difficult situations. In small doses, cortisol can be beneficial. It gives us the energy we need to get through tough times.

However, when cortisol levels are constantly high, it can lead to health problems, including heart disease, stroke, anxiety, depression and more. So even a little bit of stress is not suitable for you.

In our fast-paced world, it's easy to believe that stress is just a normal part of life. But it's not! Stress is your body's way of telling you that something is wrong.

It's a sign that you're not living in alignment with your values or you're taking on too much. When you're constantly stressed, it's a sign that you need to change what you think about your life.

Who is responsible for your stress?

You are!

Our thoughts, emotions and actions create all suffering. No one else is responsible for our stress. We can't control what happens to us, but we can control how we react.

Through my work with hundreds of leaders, and not least myself, I have come to see that it's not before we take responsibility for our thinking, emotions and actions when we're free.

It's not easy because we have been taught that it's someone else's responsibility, whether it's our upbringing, school system or society.

When you take responsibility for your thoughts, emotions and actions, you're no longer a victim of your circumstances. You're in control. And that's empowering! Here are some things you can do to reduce stress:

- Get rid of perfectionism: You are not what you do or achieve; it's something you do.
- Simplify your life: declutter your home, schedule, and make a to-do list.
- Set boundaries: learn to say "no" to things that don't align with your values or that you don't have time for.
- Spend time in nature: disconnect from technology and spend time in nature.
- Meditation is a great way to reduce stress and increase self-awareness.

We find it extremely difficult to say 'No thank you' because we need to please others, be liked and belong. Unfortunately, this need is often based on fears such as the fear of rejection or the fear of not being good enough.

You can begin questioning your thoughts and emotions when you become more aware of them. Is this true? Do I need to do this to be liked? Can I handle this situation differently?

The more you question your thoughts and emotions, the more control you will have over them. And the less they will control you! Here are some examples of thoughts to question whether they are true:

- I have to be perfect.
- I have to please everyone.
- I'm not good enough.
- I'm not worthy.
- It's not safe to relax.
- Something terrible will happen if I don't control everything.

When you become aware of the thoughts that create stress, you can start to let them go. They are just thoughts, after all. They are not reality. It's fiction.

Most problems arise from misunderstandings

We seldom meet the other where he is but where we are. It is why we so often misunderstand each other.

Have you ever met someone and walked away thinking, "Wow, that person is different from what I expected?" We've all been there. It's easy to forget that when we meet someone, we're not just meeting them - we're also meeting our story about them.

Our story is based on our past experiences, preconceptions, and assumptions. As a result, it's often more about us than the other person.

When I open myself up to another person, am I really open mindedly listening to them? Or am I just waiting for my turn to speak, so that I can share my story about them?

Most of the time, when we think we're listening to someone else, we're actually just listening to our own story about them.

We're not open-mindedly considering their thoughts and experiences - instead, we're only thinking about how those thoughts and experiences fit into our own worldview. This can lead to a lot of misunderstandings, because we're not actually communicating with the other person - we're talking to ourselves. The response we get from the other person is not at all like we had expected.

So, it's not difficult to imagine what happens when I meet my boss telling me I should have sold more. In most cases, I think he's an idiot for not understanding what I've been through the last month or few weeks.

The reality is that it's me, not my boss, who is the idiot. I've misunderstood him completely. He told me he could have better prepared the client for collaboration with our brand.

Knowing this and not believing my initial story of reality, how would I then meet my boss? With more understanding, willingness to listen and with creativity to find a solution.

Test it for yourself. Next time someone tells you what you should or should not do, think about how it could be just as accurate in characterizing the person judging you. And the other way around.

If you think someone is mean, it's because you have a story about that person being mean. But what if that person isn't mean? You're just projecting your own story onto them. So it's essential to be open-minded and self-conscious about our stories because they can often be inaccurate.

When we recognize that we're doing this, we can see people in a different light and for who they are. This will reduce stress and create better understanding, collaboration and friendship.

"Reality is merely an illusion, albeit a very persistent one" - Albert Einstein.

For example, if you grew up in a family where people were always yelling at each other, you might believe that's how all families are supposed to be. And so, when you get into a family, you might find yourself yelling at your partner and children, even though that's not how you want to be.

But if you become aware of the thoughts and emotions that are driving your behaviour, you can choose to change them. You don't have to be a victim of your past. Instead, you can create a new reality for yourself - one that is based on love, respect and understanding.

When you take responsibility for your thoughts, emotions and actions, you're no longer a victim of your circumstances. You're in control.

When we face something that challenges how we see the world, it's natural to go into fight mode. We will do whatever it takes to protect what we believe

HOW TO GET RID OF STRESS?

is the truth because we are convinced it is who we are. But what if we're open-minded enough to consider that our view of the world may not be accurate? What if we're self-conscious enough to realize that our identity is not wrapped up in our beliefs?

This doesn't mean that we should give up our convictions or stop fighting for what we believe in. But it does mean that we should be open to the possibility of being wrong.

After all, isn't that what true exploration is all about? To go beyond our comfort zone and explore new territory, even if it means admitting that we don't know everything?

The author Michael A. Singer describes it like this :

"The ego doesn't want to give up its position as the ruler of the roost, even though it's a terrible ruler. Think about how much pain and suffering you have because of your ego. It never tells you the truth; instead, it makes things up that always keep you upset."

Another example could be when your partner tells you she's unhappy with how little time she spends with you. You might feel like a victim because of all the pressure from work. Your first reaction is to get defensive and find all the reasons why it's her fault and not yours.

The reality is that both of you are right and also wrong. The truth is somewhere in between. The only way to find out is to have an open and honest conversation without getting defensive or blaming each other.

When we're caught up in our ego, we cannot see reality as it is. Instead, we see things through the lens of our own biases, assumptions and experiences. It can lead us to react in ways that are not helpful or productive and can even make our problems worse.

The key to freedom and fewer misunderstandings is self-consciousness. We can start questioning our thoughts and emotions when we know them. Is this true? Do I need to do this to be liked? Can I handle this situation differently?

However, when we become aware that thoughts and emotions are just visitors in our minds, we can see them for what they are: Temporary and ever-changing. We are not our thoughts or emotions. We are the Awareness that is watching them.

By increasing our self-consciousness, we can see reality as it is without the filters of our ego. As a result, we can become more flexible in our thinking and responding and find more creative solutions to our problems. We can also develop more compassion for ourselves and others as we realize that we are all just human beings struggling to make sense of our lives.

So the next time you find yourself caught up in your ego, remember that you are not your thoughts or emotions. You are the Awareness that is watching them. And from this place of Awareness, you can choose how you want to respond to any situation.

It's crucial to use I-messages to avoid misunderstandings. These are non-judgemental messages focused on how we feel.

For example: "I feel frustrated when you're late for our meeting" rather than "You're always late, and it's so disrespectful."

The first message opens a constructive dialogue because it doesn't put the person on the defensive. Instead, it focuses on how you feel, not what the person did wrong.

The other person is not the problem - our interpretation of reality creates the confusion.

Being angry makes you believe everything

I came across some research conducted by Michael Greenstein, an assistant professor at Framingham State University. Greenstein's research focuses on how people respond to misinformation, and in particular, how their emotions can impact their ability to discern between fact and fiction.

One of the most interesting findings from Greenstein's research is that people are more likely to believe misinformation when they are angry. This is likely due to the fact that angry people tend to be more confident in their convictions, even when those convictions are based on false information.

Additionally, Greenstein found that people are more likely to believe misinformation that aligns with their prior beliefs. This suggests that we are all susceptible to falling prey to fake news, especially if it reinforces our existing worldview.

Greenstein's research provides valuable insights into how fake news proliferates and how we can best protect ourselves from being misled by it. In today's age of information overload, it is more important than ever to be aware of the impact our emotions can have on our ability to judge what is true and what is false.

When I watch what is happening globally, outrage content spreads the farthest and fastest.

The research is conclusive. Joy moves faster than sadness or disgust, but nothing is speedier than rage. We all know a specific person who has taken advantage of this insight for a long time.

It's not the algorithms that cause us to form into hordes of mad people —it's merely biased human cognition. We tend to remember and believe what upsets us, regardless of whether it is true. We tend to be more confident in our beliefs of what bothered us, especially if it isn't true.

Anger likely causes us to believe self-preserving things, even if they are unreal. Therefore, it makes sense to be alert to the information which makes you angry.

A way to double pass this cognitive effect is to become aware of what makes you angry and ask yourself if you can be 100 % sure it's the truth you believe in and how your life would be without this belief.

CHAPTER 8
Welcome to earth school

We come into this life with fresh eyes and open minds, ready to learn all we can in the time we have. Along the way, we are taught by those around us – our parents, teachers, friends, and others.

Sometimes what we learn is straightforward; other times, it's more complex and takes longer to understand.

But no matter what we learn, each piece of knowledge shapes who we believe we are as individuals. And as we continue to learn and grow mentally and emotionally, we see that everything is connected.

All of the things we experience – both good and bad – have the potential to help us become wiser and more compassionate people. So even though it may seem like life is one big test or struggle, remember that you are always learning something new and attending earth school.

Teachers surround us

And let's be thankful for all the fantastic teachers who surround us daily!

We are constantly surrounded by teachers, even when we don't realize it. The person who cuts you off in traffic and makes you honk in anger? They're teaching you patience (or lack thereof).

The colleague who G-chats you non-stop about their weekend? They're teaching you boundaries.

Even that friend who always cancels plans last minute? They're teaching you how to be more reliable.

Of course, not all of these examples are positive - but they're all teachable moments nonetheless.

Good leaders know this and embrace learning from others, regardless of how much they may have to teach them.

Great leaders know those excellent teachers are also good students - a quality that is sometimes forgotten in the hustle and bustle of everyday life. By remaining curious and learning from those around us, we can continuously grow and improve - both as individuals and as a society.

It's often said that we learn more from our failures than our successes. But learning from our mistakes isn't just about learning from bad experiences. It's also about learning from good ones. After all, the best teachers are also good students.

It was borne out by a recent study by researchers at the University of Toronto. The study found that people who are curious and open to learning new things are more likely to be successful than those who aren't.

So, if you feel like you're surrounded by idiots, take heart. We're all teachers and students, and the best way to learn is to be curious and open-minded.

Who knows? You might learn something from even the most stupid among us.

It's curious why learning from people we don't like is so difficult. After all, learning is supposed to be an open-minded process where we're willing to explore new ideas and grow as individuals.

When we don't like someone, it's often much harder to listen to what they say. Instead, we get wrapped up in our biases and preconceptions and find it hard to hear what the other person is saying sincerely. As a result, we can take advantage of vital learning opportunities.

So next time you find yourself in a situation where you don't particularly like the person you're talking to, try to be open-minded and curious - you might just be surprised at what you learn.

What you don't know, you know

We like to think that we know things. We go to school to learn facts and figure out how the world works. But often, what we think we know is only part of the story.

In a recent Harvard Business Review article, learning expert Josh Kaufman argues that we don't know something until we can apply it in a real-world situation.

Kaufman writes that learning consists of three stages:

- cognition (understanding the concept),
- activation (putting the idea into practice),

- integration (incorporating the concept into your existing knowledge).

Learning is essential, but what makes us experts in our field is the tacit knowledge we have. This knowledge is not explicitly taught but is gleaned through experience and observation.

As Robert Sapolsky, a professor at Stanford, puts it: "That's the kind of learning where you assimilate procedural know-how so thoroughly, that it becomes second nature and doesn't even rise to the level of conscious awareness."

This kind of learning allows us to instinctively know how to do things, ultimately making us experts in our respective fields. So when you're curious about something, don't be afraid to ask questions and explore. Again, it's learning that will make you an expert.

Albert Einstein, one of the most brilliant minds of our time, had a lot to say about learning. He once said, "I never teach my pupils. I only attempt to provide the conditions in which they can learn."

In other words, he believed that learning was not something that could be taught - instead, it was something that students had to engage in for themselves.

It is still true today. Learning requires curiosity and a willingness to explore. It can't be forced or dictated - instead, it must be embraced by the learner. It is why Einstein's quote remains relevant today. Learning is an active process that begins with a willingness to be curious and open-minded.

Meet your fundamental beliefs

Most of us go through life without thinking about what we believe and how those beliefs colour our world experience.

But if we take a moment to reflect, we may be surprised to discover how much our beliefs influence how we see and interact with the world.

Simply put, our beliefs are the lens through which we view reality. They shape the way we learn, interpret information, and make decisions. Our beliefs can even affect our physical health!

It's interesting to think about how our fundamental beliefs affect our lives. For example, do we believe that we're worthy of love? That we're deserving of good things? Or do we think the opposite -

that we're not good enough, that we'll never be able to achieve our goals?

Byron Katie's work suggests that our beliefs profoundly affect how we experience life. For example, if we believe we're not good enough, we'll go through life feeling anxious and inferior. We'll miss out on opportunities because we don't think we deserve them. We'll stay in relationships that aren't healthy for us because we don't think we can do any better.

Learning to question our beliefs is essential in creating a life that feels good to us. When we're curious about our beliefs, we open ourselves up to the possibility of change. We can examine the evidence for and against our thoughts and decide whether or not they're serving us. If not, we can let them go and Replace them with something more empowering.

Most of us have at least one fundamental belief that holds us back. For example, you might believe you can't get a job because you're 50 + years old.

This belief can be deeply ingrained, but the moment you question the thought that you can't find a new job because of your age, you will see that you can't be 100 % sure that is true.

And without that, your age has nothing to do with you finding it difficult to land a new job. Instead, you will have a clearer mind and curiosity to approach interesting companies you can help from A to B.

However, Byron Katie's work can help. Katie encourages people to learn about their fundamental beliefs and to be curious about them.

This process can reveal that these beliefs may need to be revised. As a result, you can let go of the belief and open yourself up to new possibilities. Who knows - learning about your fundamental beliefs could improve your life.

We don't own anything

We live in a world where we're constantly being told that we need to buy things. Even our clothes send a message that we're not good enough unless we wear the latest fashion.

But what if we took a step back and realized that we don't own anything? It's true! We may possess material items, but they don't belong to us. Instead, everything is simply on loan.

We tend to think of our belongings as extensions of ourselves - after all, they are a part of our daily lives, and we see them daily. But what if we looked at our things differently? What if, instead of seeing them as ours, we saw them as something we have had for a time?

It may seem like a slight shift in perspective, but it can significantly impact how we view ourselves.

We can also be more mindful of how we use and care for them. When we see our things this way, we can begin to let go of the idea that we need to hold on to everything forever, which we can't. Instead, we can appreciate the temporary nature of our possessions and the stories we tell ourselves about our old red cars.

CHAPTER 9

Without your story, who are you?

It's no secret that we all live with some degree of fear. Whether it's fear for our safety, the safety of our loved ones, or simply the anxiety of everyday life. Fear is a constant presence in our lives.

But what if I told you that much of the fear we experience is generated by our minds? That's right; research has shown that a significant portion of our fear is based on an imagined threat that we believe to be real. And not only that, but this process of learning to be afraid is something we're hardwired for.

From a young age, we're constantly learning about the world around us and what to be afraid of.

Just think about the last time you saw a scary movie or heard a frightening story. What happened? Your brain starts generating images and scenarios based on what you saw and heard. And while these may have been purely fictional, your mind didn't know. As a result, you experience fear because your brain thinks you are in danger.

So the next time you feel afraid, remember that it may just be your mind playing tricks on you. And instead of letting fear control your life, take a step back and ask yourself if there's anything to be afraid of.

After all, learning to question our fears is essential to living a happy and fulfilling life.

It's interesting how our minds work. We can be sure of something and yet be entirely wrong.

We can convince ourselves that we are in danger, even when there is no threat. And sometimes, what we fear most happens, and we find out that there is nothing to fear. We learn that the things we were so sure of were entirely false.

We realized that our minds had been playing tricks on us and that the danger was only in our heads. It's a scary feeling but can also be a learning experience.

After all, if we can be wrong about something we were so sure of, what else might we be wrong about? It can be a humbling experience, but it can also make us more curious and open-minded. And that's not a bad thing.

We're terrified of only two things: losing what we have and not getting what we want. It was famously articulated by Byron Katie, who said that "everything we do is because we think it's going to bring us happiness."

Fear is simply a byproduct of our desire for happiness. We're afraid of losing the things that make us happy, and we're scared of not being able to obtain the things that will make us happy.

Ultimately, learning to live with fear is a matter of learning to live with uncertainty. We can't control everything in our lives and trying to do so is ultimately futile.

Instead, the key is staying curious and open-minded and remembering that happiness always lurks around the corner. Who knows? The thing you're afraid of might end up being the best thing ever happening to you.

No one needs to like me.

We all want to be loved.

What happens when we believe that other people need to love us for us to love ourselves?

We may start to see ourselves negatively, thinking we're not good enough or don't deserve love. As a result, we may begin putting up walls, physically and emotionally, to protect ourselves from getting hurt.

Alternatively, we may act in ways designed to elicit love and approval from others, even if it means sacrificing our own needs and wants. Either way, we close ourselves off from the possibility of truly learning to love ourselves.

Instead, we end up living in a state of fear, insecurity, and self-doubt.

Michael A. Singer, in his book "The Untethered Soul", challenges us to think about our relationship to happiness.

He asks: "Who are you? The one who is aware of learning or is learning?" In other words, are we the observer of our own lives, or are we caught up in the drama of everyday existence?

He argues that we can be happy only when we step back and take an objective view of our lives. It is because our happiness has nothing to do with other people loving us, but rather our capacity to love ourselves. If we don't love ourselves, how can others? If we learn to love ourselves, we will be happy no matter what happens.

Why have we come to believe that we are not worth loving? It seems like such a crazy idea when you think about it.

We are all born of love; it's our very nature. So what could lead us to believe we are not worthy of love?

It could be argued that it's simply a matter of learning. As we grow up and experience the world, we see that some people are loved, and others are not. From this, we can infer that something about us must make us unlovable.

We may not be funny, pretty, or intelligent enough. This line of thinking can become a self-fulfilling prophecy - if we believe we're not worth loving, we'll act in ways that reinforce that belief. Others will pick up on our low self-worth and treat us accordingly.

But there's also another possibility. We may believe we're not worth loving because we've never really stopped to think about it. We've never looked at ourselves through the lens of love and asked ourselves whether or not we deserve it.

Instead, we've accepted the love of others as a given and gone through life without considering our worthiness. If this is the case, it's time to start being curious about ourselves.

Why do we deserve love? What makes us lovable? When we start asking these questions, we might be surprised by what we discover about ourselves. We might find that we are worthy of love - just as we have always been.

There is nothing new, just repetition

There is some truth to the statement that "there's nothing new under the sun." Many problems are simply repeated in different contexts. However, we can still learn from past experiences and find new ways to address old issues.

Humans often find it challenging to learn from their mistakes instead of repeating them; this may be due to several factors, such as cognitive biases and limitations in our memories. For instance, we may be more likely to remember information that confirms our beliefs than information that challenges them, leading us to make inaccurate judgments.

Additionally, our memories are often inaccurate representations of past events, so we may not learn from experiences we don't remember accurately.

By being aware of the patterns in our lives, we can work to prevent them from repeating themselves.

According to the renowned author and speaker, Wayne Dyer, "You'll see that change comes from changing the story you tell yourself."

We must first change our perspective to create a new story for ourselves. Then, when we change our viewpoint, we can begin learning about and understanding ourselves in a new way.

We can do this by looking at our past experiences and acknowledging the lessons we have learned from them. We can also look at the people in our lives and appreciate the lessons they have taught us. Doing this allows us to see ourselves in a new light and cultivate a more positive story.

When we change the story we tell ourselves, we change our lives. So, next time you find yourself in a situation that feels all too familiar and creates stress, take a step back and see if there is anything new you can learn from it or if you are repeating a behaviour that doesn't serve you well. Chances are, there is.

You are your ghostwriter, so you change the world when you change the story.

CHAPTER 10

When nothing is going your way

According to Peter M. Senge, "The only way to achieve flow is to learn how to go with the flow." In other words, we must learn to accept reality and work with it instead of against it. It's a difficult task for most of us, as we are conditioned to resist what is happening and try to control the outcome. However, as Michael A. Singer points out, "fighting against reality only creates more suffering."

So why is it better for us to go with the flow?

First, by accepting reality, we can focus on what is happening in the present moment rather than on what we want or don't want. It allows us to respond more effectively to the situation at hand.

Second, by working with reality, we open ourselves up to opportunities and possibilities that would not be available if we were trying to control everything.

Finally, by going with the flow, we reduce stress and anxiety, which allows us to be more creative and productive.

When we understand that the challenges in our lives are not happening to us but rather FOR us, it can change everything. We can see these challenges as opportunities for growth and expansion. It's a decisive shift in perspective that can open up a world of possibilities.

Peter M. Senge, the author of The Fifth Discipline, says, "The only way to grow is to be willing to risk failure." When we're willing to face our challenges head-on, we're opening ourselves up to the possibility of learning and growing from them.

Michael A. Singer, the author of The Untethered Soul, says, "When you finally recognise that all those things you once thought were problems were just part of the process of becoming who you are meant to be, then you can relax."

We can feel upset and frustrated when things don't go our way. It's often because we have developed an idea of how we want things to be, and when reality doesn't match that idea, we can experience a great deal of dissonance.

According to Peter M. Senge, "we make assumptions about how the world works and then try to bend reality to fit our assumptions." In other words, our expectations or mental models can often lead us astray.

So when we encounter a challenge in our lives, instead of seeing it as a negative experience, we can see it as an opportunity for growth and expansion. We can embrace it as part of becoming who we are. It's a powerful way to live and bring happiness and peace of mind.

When something we want doesn't happen to us, it can be challenging to understand what that means. Events that we consider bad luck could be seen as good news from a different perspective.

The fact that we got laid off might be the best thing to have happened to us because it forced us to find new opportunities. Our boyfriend finding another girlfriend might be the best thing for him because it allows him to find someone who is better suited to him. And someone stealing our bike might be a good thing because it encourages us to buy a new one.

All of these things might not seem like they're going our way at first, but if we look at them from a different perspective, we can see they're happening for us. So even when something seems like bad luck, it's working in our favour.

Senge recommends focusing on the process instead of becoming attached to specific outcomes. We take an interest in what we're doing and how we're doing it, regardless of the outcome. When we do this, we're less likely to get upset when things don't go our way, and we're more likely to learn and grow from our experiences.

Senge says, "we usually experience the greatest dissonance when our mental model is violated by new information that doesn't fit our preconceptions."

So, when our mental models are violated by new information, it can be difficult to accept because it doesn't fit our preconceptions. Our preconceptions may have been formed from our personal experiences or based on what we have been taught.

When new information contradicts what we believe, it can create a lot of dissonance. This dissonance can cause us to become upset because it feels like our world is crashing down around us. We may feel like we can't trust our judgment anymore, which can be very unsettling.

However, it is important to remember that our mental models are just that - models. They are unreal and can be changed or updated when new information becomes available.

In these cases, it's essential to be open to the possibility that our initial understanding may have been wrong and that the new information could offer a better understanding of what's happening. Only by being open to this possibility can we learn and grow from our experiences.

How to win the war against yourselves?

Humans are constantly at war with themselves; they must take sides to defeat themselves. To lead ourselves in this war, we must first know what we should and want. However, this is not always easy, as it requires us to be honest with ourselves and acknowledge our weaknesses and shortcomings. It's often tricky, but it is crucial if we want to live our lives in a way that is authentic and fulfilling.

The human mind is not fragile; in fact, it is resilient. However, if we don't face reality and instead try to protect ourselves by telling ourselves stories worse than reality, we don't healthily grow our minds.

It can be seen in the example of a young child who is repeatedly told that the world is dangerous.

As a result, the child may start to believe that the world is scary, which can hinder their development.

Another example can be seen in the case of someone who has been through a traumatic experience. Although this person doesn't face up to the occasion and instead tells herself a story in which she is the victim, she may never fully recover from the trauma. Therefore, it is important to face reality head-on so we can grow our minds healthily.

According to Herbert Simon, one of the founders of artificial intelligence, humans are not rational decision-makers.

Our decision-making is bounded by the amount of information available at any given time. It's why we often make poor decisions or seem irrational - our brains are just trying to make the best decisions possible with the information we have available. Our brain is guessing. It doesn't know anything.

It means that if we can increase our understanding of a situation, we can make better decisions.

It's good news for those who struggle with inner conflict because it means that by increasing our understanding of ourselves and our situations, we can make better decisions and resolve our internal wars.

To overcome these inner conflicts, we must be honest with ourselves and learn to accept ourselves for who we are becoming.

Self-leadership is an essential factor in overall success. In a study of nearly 200 business professionals, those who reported high levels of self-leadership also reported higher levels of career satisfaction and job performance (Harvey, Newman, & Ciarrochi, 2014).

Additionally, self-leadership is an essential predictor of goal achievement. For example, in a study of nearly 300 college students, those who scored high in self-leadership were more likely to achieve their academic goals (Gardner, Saklofske, & Zeidner, 2003).

There are many reasons why self-leadership is vital for achieving success.

First, self-leadership allows individuals to stay focused on their goals and priorities. Individuals with solid self-leadership skills can regulate their thoughts and behaviours and stay on track despite distractions or setbacks.

Second, self-leadership enables individuals to take the initiative and be proactive. Individuals with solid self-leadership skills are not afraid to take action and seize opportunities when they arise.

Finally, self-leadership promotes independence and autonomy. Individuals with solid self-leadership skills can make decisions independently and chart their life course.

Olympic athletes often talk about the importance of self-leadership in achieving their goals. Michael Phelps, for example, has said, "I had to learn to be my coach because no one else was going to do it for me."

When you realize that you are the best friend you could wish for, you will never be alone. Instead, you will have someone to rely on in good and bad times. It's because you understand yourself and your needs so well. You know how to comfort and support others, making you a valuable friend.

You are also comfortable with yourself. It means you don't need external validation or approval to feel good about yourself.

This inner peace allows you to be there for your friends without expecting anything in return. You are indeed a gift to anyone who knows you!

To show dignity to yourself

It becomes tough to meet others with dignity if we don't satisfy ourselves with dignity. We may be demanding or entitled, expecting respect without giving it first. It can lead to frustration and resentment in our interactions with others. For example, I have observed parents who wish their children would show respect but do not model that behaviour themselves. As a result, the children inevitably rebel and end up disrespectful.

I have also seen people get angry when they are not treated the way they want(expect?), without considering how they have previously treated others.

It is essential to be aware of our behaviour and treat others with the same respect we would like to be treated with too. It becomes challenging to meet and treat others with dignity, if we don't meet ourselves with dignity.

We may be demanding or entitled, expecting respect without giving it first. It can lead to frustration and resentment in our interactions with others.

People often fall into a pattern of negativity and self-criticism, which can be damaging not only to our psyche but to our relationships with others.

Being kind and gentle with ourselves sets the tone for how we approach the world. We are more likely to be patient and understanding with others and to see the best in them. We are also more likely to care for ourselves physically and emotionally. Treating ourselves with dignity creates a foundation for happiness and fulfillment in our lives.

When are we genuinely kind and gentle towards ourselves? Is it when we are in the moment, present with whatever is happening?

Or is it when we allow ourselves to be present with what is happening, even if it isn't what we want?

Eckhart Tolle would say that it is the latter. He believes our essential nature is one of kindness and love, but we are not always in touch with that part of ourselves. Instead, we often focus on the ego, which can lead to thoughts and actions that are anything but kind and gentle.

However, when we can quiet the ego and connect with our true nature, we can act from a place of kindness and love. Of course, this doesn't mean that everything will be perfect or that we will always make the right decisions, but it does mean that we will be more in tune with our hearts and more able to care for ourselves and others in a way that is genuinely kind and gentle.

Let go

In his book, *The Embodied Mind*, cognitive scientist Francisco Varela explores the idea that we need to let go to experience life truly. He argues that our need to control everything around us prevents us from being open to new experiences.

Instead, we become attached to our ideas and beliefs and close ourselves off from anything that might challenge them. It can limit our ability to grow and learn and prevent us from truly connecting with others. Only by letting go of our need to control can we be free to explore the world without attachment or fear.

Of course, this doesn't mean we should abandon all structure and order. But it does mean that we should be open to new ideas and experiences without feeling the need to control them; only then can we truly learn and grow.

THE TIPPING POINT

It was the most devastating day of my life when I learned that my twin brother had died in an accident. We were only 23 years old. I felt like I couldn't go on without him. We were so close; we did everything together. But then something unique happened. Out of my grief, I discovered that I could still live without him and be happy for my life.

I felt I was still me, even without my other half. It was a revelation to me. I realized that I was not defined by my relationship with someone else but by my consciousness. And without attachment, I found freedom. It was a turning point, leading me to a life of greater joy and fulfillment than I ever thought possible.

We all have those days when nothing goes right. It's a frustrating experience to try and fix what seems broken in your life, only for things to get even more complicated than before we started trying.

But, the moment we move away from the chaos and get still, just persevering on what's going on, the stressful thoughts start to let go of us, and we can begin to act with more clarity.

Listen with your heart

Have you ever found yourself so caught up in your head, analysing and overthinking every little detail of a situation, that you forgot to listen to your heart?

We've all been there. We get so used to living life from our heads that we forget there's another way. But what if I told you that by learning to listen with your heart, you would not only get to know yourself on a deeper level but also let go of old beliefs and attitudes that no longer serve you?

When we experience life from our heads, we constantly attach meaning to everything that happens to us. We interpret every event as good or bad, right or wrong, and then we hold onto these interpretations without realizing it. This can lead us to rigid beliefs about who we are and how the world works. But we can see things differently when we experience life from our hearts instead of our heads.

We can let go of the need to interpret everything and allow ourselves to take a chance on serendipity. And when we do this, we open ourselves up to a new way of being in the world.

So how do you start listening with your heart? The first step is to become aware of when you're doing it. Pay attention when you are overthinking or getting caught up in your head.

Once you become aware of when it's happening, remind yourself that you have a choice: keep going down the same old rabbit hole or bring your attention back to your heart.

It takes practice, but the more you do it, the easier it will become. And before long, you'll see life in a whole new light, just as I did when Kim, my twin brother, died.

CHAPTER 11

The power of vulnerability

What is vulnerability? Why do we feel it? Is it a good thing or a bad thing?

There is no single answer to these questions. Vulnerability is a complex and nuanced emotion that can be experienced in different ways by different people. For some, vulnerability may be experienced as a sense of openness and receptivity. This can be a positive feeling, associated with trust, intimacy, and connection. For others, vulnerability may be experienced as a sense of exposure or insecurity. This can be a negative feeling, associated with anxiety, fear, and helplessness.

There is no right or wrong way to feel vulnerable. What matters is how we react to and manage our feelings of vulnerability. When we are able to embrace our vulnerabilities, we open ourselves up to the possibility of growth, love, and connection.

When we allow our vulnerabilities to control us, we may miss out on important opportunities or end up feeling even more isolated and alone.

So the next time you feel vulnerable, ask yourself: what am I feeling and why? How can I use this feeling to my advantage?

By understanding and accepting our vulnerabilities, we can learn to better navigate the challenges and relationships of our lives.

Recently, we've seen a shift in how people talk about their vulnerabilities.

Where once sharing our vulnerabilities was seen as a sign of weakness, today, it's increasingly viewed as a strength. But why is this? What has led so many of us to open up about our vulnerabilities? And what do our vulnerabilities mean for us?

There are several reasons why we share our vulnerabilities today. For one, we live in an increasingly connected world where it's easier than ever to reach out to others and build relationships. This connection can be a source of strength, especially when we're going through tough times.

Additionally, as we've become more aware of mental health issues, we've come to understand that vulnerability is a normal part of the human experience. This understanding has helped reduce the stigma around vulnerability and encourage more people to speak openly about their struggles.

Furthermore, sharing our vulnerabilities can help build trust and intimacy in our relationships. When we open up about our fears and what we believe to be weaknesses, we permit others to do the same. This leads to deeper connections and a sense of shared humanity. Additionally, when we're honest about our vulnerabilities, we're more likely to receive support and compassion from ourselves and others.

Finally, sharing our vulnerabilities can be empowering. It can help us regain control of our lives after feeling like we've been holding everything together for too long.

While being vulnerable has many benefits, some risks are also involved.

The most significant risk is that we may be met with judgment or rejection from others. This is not easy to cope with, especially if we've opened up about something important.

In addition, vulnerability can sometimes lead to feeling overwhelmed or out of control. But this is because opening up about our struggles can make them feel more natural or intense.

However, there are ways to manage these risks. For example, carefully choosing who you open up to is essential. Make sure it's someone you trust and who you know will be supportive.

Setting boundaries is essential in maintaining healthy relationships, both with others and with ourselves. By setting clear boundaries, we are able to protect our physical and emotional well-being from being overextended or taken advantage of.

When we establish boundaries, we are also teaching others how to treat us. If we allow others to constantly invade our personal space or repeatedly neglect our boundaries, we are effectively telling them that their behaviour is acceptable.

On the other hand, when we hold firm to our boundaries, we are sending the message that we expect to be treated with respect.

It is only when we nurture a culture of respect for boundaries that we can create healthy, meaningful relationships with those around us.

Finally, knowing that when you share the moments you feel vulnerable, with people, and they don't react as you had envisioned, it has nothing to do with you. So don't take it personally.

If you have a friend or loved one who is opening up about their vulnerabilities, there are a few things you can do to support them:

1. Listen without judgment or advice-giving. Just let them know that you're here for them and that you understand what they're going through.
2. Offer practical help if they need it but don't try to take over or fix their problems; they need to do this themselves as part of the healing process.
3. Remind them. They're not alone in this; many people struggle with similar issues.

Reassure them that they will get through this tough time and come out stronger on the other side.

Seek, and you shall find happiness

The pursuit of happiness is a central tenet of many cultures around the world. For example, the ancient Greek philosopher Aristotle famously said that "happiness is the meaning and the purpose of life, the whole aim and end of human existence." The Stoic philosopher Seneca echoed this sentiment, writing that "every man seeks happiness."

In recent years, happiness has become a fundamental human right. So what does this all mean for our experience of joy?

The idea that happiness is something to be pursued is deeply ingrained in our collective consciousness. But what does it mean to pursue happiness? And what are the implications of this pursuit? Pursuing happiness can be daunting because it often seems an elusive goal.

What is the meaning of life? Is it to be happy and free from suffering? If so, why do we often seek things that we know will only make us suffer in the long run?

For instance, when we believe happiness can increase by eating three desserts instead of one, we will always lack happiness because we think more is better.

The fact is, however, that most things in life are best experienced in moderation. Conversely, seemingly innocuous as dessert, too much of anything will lead to problems.

Everybody is searching for the meaning of life in the wrong places. But what if the answer is more straightforward than we think?

The meaning of life may be just the total of our individual experiences. The highs and lows, the good days and the bad days. The things that make us laugh and the things that make us cry.

The off days are a valuable part of this equation. They provide us with a chance to step back and assess our lives. Take stock of what's going well and what could be going better. To reflect on our choices and think about the options we still have to make. Off days are like reboots for our souls. They help us to remember what's important and keep us moving forward on our journey.

So next time you feel down, see it as an opportunity for growth and reflection. You might find the meaning of life in the process.

It is interesting to explore the concept that many leaders believe to be true: Without a title, no identity. And with no identity, no meaning in life.

Some leaders appear to be attached to their titles and the power that comes with them.

However, upon closer inspection, it might be possible to see that these leaders are using their position to cover up a deep-seated insecurity.

Perhaps they feel they are only worthy of love or respect if they have an impressive title. Or maybe they are afraid to be themselves, so they use their title to create a persona they can hide behind.

Whatever the case, it is clear that for these leaders, their title is more than just a label – it is a deeply ingrained part of their identity. Without it, they feel lost and uncertain.

It raises the question: What is the meaning of life if we are not living in the present moment? If our sense of self is wrapped up in our titles and achievements, we miss life's beauty.

We are not truly living – we are just going through the motions. To truly live, we must be conscious of the now. We must let go of our attachment to our titles and past accomplishments and be present in each moment. That is when we will find true meaning and happiness in life.

Courage to live

It's interesting how we can be going along in life, seemingly stuck in a rut, and suddenly, something happens that completely changes our perspective. It's like the fog lifts, and we can see clearly again.

We may have been trying to force something to happen or to will our way out of a situation, but it's only when we let go and surrender to what it is, that things begin to shift. We may not always see how things will work out, but if we have faith, anything is possible.

It is interesting to note that Van Gogh had a two-year period in which he didn't paint. He instead spent his time mixing colours, feeling that he was wasting his time because he wasn't painting. However, this turned out to be a very fertile period for him, as he painted with enormous energy and creativity once he resumed.

This shows that even when we are not making progress, we may be laying the groundwork for something great. So don't give up - even if you're stuck in a rut, you never know what might be around the corner.

I think there is value in considering: what if "what is" is the plan?

Rather than trying to seize control of our lives, what if we simply allowed things to unfold as they may? This doesn't mean that we shouldn't take action when it's warranted, but rather that we should not get attached to how things should be or look. When we let go of our expectations, we open ourselves to new possibilities and experiences. We become more curious about what shows up rather than fixating on what we think should be happening.

So next time you feel stressed or anxious about an upcoming event, try asking yourself, "what if what is, is the plan?"

It might help you to let go of your attachment to the outcome and allow yourself to enjoy the ride.

What if it's not a coincidence who we meet in life? Are we then more curious about what we could learn from the people we meet?

The answer may vary from person to person. However, we would all be more inquisitive and take the time to get to know each individual if we thought there was a greater purpose behind the meeting.

We could pay more attention to the stories they have to share and the lessons they could teach us. In turn, we would be more open-minded and compassionate towards others, seeing them not as strangers but as potential friends and mentors.

I've had my fair share of bad leaders and, as a result, learned much about what not to do.

One day, I decided that instead of wallowing in my troubles, I would turn them into learning opportunities. I decided that when I became a leader,

I would do the opposite of what I had experienced and lead people with compassion and respect. By doing this, I've learned from everything I've encountered and become a better leader.

Our encounters with others may be part of some grand plan to help us learn and grow.

What if, instead of fearing what could go wrong, we embraced the idea that nothing can go wrong?

What if we decided to live with courage and trust that everything would work out in the end?

What would our lives look like then?

For starters, we worry a lot less. We would be more likely to take risks and follow our dreams, knowing that no matter what happened, we would be okay.

We would also be more present in each moment, enjoying the good times and trusting that the bad times will pass. In short, we would be living life more fully.

CHAPTER 12

Be the difference you want to see

The moments when I have been happiest are when I have helped others achieve something. It could be as simple as making kids laugh who were sick, helping a stranger, being present for my parents or helping my friends.

You may also know the feeling of seeing another person's gratitude or light in their eyes from a small gesture from you.

The moments where I have been most sad have been when I have blamed others for not being as I would like them to be. It is very egocentric to believe that people need to be a certain way for me to be happy.

Blaming others puts me in a victim mindset and keeps me from taking responsibility for my happiness. I now understand that no one needs to change to be happy—when I change, the world changes. Instead of blaming others, I focus on what

I can change about myself and my situation. This has helped me to feel more empowered and happier overall.

The quote "Be the difference you want to see in the world" is often attributed to Mahatma Gandhi, although there is some dispute about whether he said it. Whoever first said it, the sentiment is a powerful one.

It speaks to the idea that we each have the power to make a positive difference in the world simply by being our best selves.

In other words, we don't need to wait for somebody else to change things; we can start making a difference simply by living our lives with integrity and focus. When we set an example of what it looks like to be kind, compassionate and deliberate, we may inspire others to do the same.

Making a difference in the world is not just about feel-good moments or making other people happy. It's about knowing yourself and what you're capable of. It's about feeling like you're part of something larger than yourself.

And it's about making a positive impact on the world around you.

The world needs it!

Whether volunteering your time to help those in need or simply listening to a friend in need, making a difference is everything. It's an essential part of who we are as human beings and something we should all strive for.

Lead from within

We can all be leaders by simply being the change we want to see in the world. It starts with knowing ourselves and being aware that when we meet another, we meet our story about the other, which means we meet ourselves! In knowing ourselves, we become more compassionate and curious about others. From this place, we can have the opportunity to co-create with others instead of competing.

When we act from a place of knowing ourselves, we are less likely to get reactive and judgmental towards others.

We can also be more present to spot opportunities to serve others and the world around us.

In knowing ourselves, we realize that everything is connected and that our leadership is not just about us but also something much bigger than ourselves.

Making a difference in the world is not just about feel good moments or making other people happy. It's about knowing yourself and what you're capable of. It's about feeling like you're part of something larger than yourself. And it's about making a positive impact on the world around you. Whether volunteering your time to help those in need or simply listening to a friend in need, making a difference is everything. It's an essential part of who we are as human beings and something we should all strive for.

When we lead from this place, it becomes easier to inspire others to do the same. It all starts with yourself. So ask yourself: who do you want to be in the world? And then go out and be that person!

People are naturally drawn to follow when we lead from this place of compassion and wisdom. Because they can see that we are living our truth and are genuinely committed to making a difference in the world.

Playing the wrong role

When you play a game that doesn't feel right because you're trying to play a role other than the one you want, it's hard to play it for long.

I have noticed, about myself and listening to my customers' stories, that the chain jumps off when we are not true to what we stand for in our hearts.

Often our ego drowns out our inner voice and 'makes' us put ourselves on cruise control and howl as if we were among wolves, many of whom are much better at howling than we are.

The sociologist Charles Horton Cooley wrote in 1902: "I am not what I think I am, and I am not what you think I am. I am what I think you think I am."

It's the kind of sentence that needs to be read a few times and requires some inner silence to digest. Our self-image is governed by what others think of us or what we think others think of us. And we are swamped trying to live up to this imaginary image of an ideal, often at our values' expense.

When we become aware that our ego fills us with gossip and that we don't need to be tone-deaf to our inner voice, the fear of stepping up, stepping alongside, and stepping into character evaporates.

The transformation at work often starts with us, under the radar, practicing being more aware of our behaviour because that is how we can see how we can benefit from an even more significant change in the organisation.

All real change starts with yourself and your behaviour:

- The way you meet colleagues.
- The way you call meetings.
- The way you stop and listen.
- The way you ask questions.
- The way you feel, whether what you are overly aware of is right, is now the truth.
- The way you look after yourself.
- The way you meet yourself.

Exercise

Do you ever find yourself pursuing tasks or striving for a specific image out of obligation rather than passion? It's essential to take a step back from time to time and ask yourselves three key questions:

1. What is my underlying motivation for each action I'm taking?
2. Does it help me reach goals that reflect who I am?
3. Which path will be best suited for my growth in the long run?

Discovering your original purpose requires introspection and understanding how your believed external pressures can shape your choices, regardless of whether they can be false.

What do you truly want? This question can be difficult to answer, as we are often bombarded with messages from society telling us what we should want.

However, it is essential to take the time to reflect on what we truly desire, as this can help us to lead more fulfilling lives. There are many ways to figure out what we want, but one of the most important is to listen to our hearts.Our heart knows what we need, even if our mind doesn't understand it.

Trusting our hearts can be scary, but it is often the best way to find our true path in life. When we find what we truly want, we often feel a sense of peace and clarity.

We will know that this is what we are meant to do or have, and everything will fall into place. It may not be easy, but following our hearts is often the best way to achieve lasting happiness.

When more than being intelligent is needed

Intelligence has always been heralded as the highest ideal to aspire to. After all, it is the one quality we can all hope to improve through study and practice.

However, there are times when more than being intelligent is needed.

There are times when wisdom is required. Wisdom is the ability to see the world clearly and make sound judgments. It is the ability to view situations from multiple perspectives and find the best action.

Wisdom is not a static quality; it must be actively cultivated. Unfortunately, there are no wisdom schools or wisdom degrees. wisdom must be sought out through life experience and thoughtful reflection.

If there is one school for wisdom, it's Earth School.

Many people often ask the question, what is wisdom? Wisdom, according to Google, is the quality of having experience, knowledge, and good judgment; the quality of being wise.

But modern-day philosophers have their definition of wisdom. For example, philosophers theorized that "Wisdom is seeing things as they are." In other words, it is seeing the world for what it is instead of what we want it to be.

While this may be a difficult task, it is an important one. After all, wisdom is essential for making good decisions in life.

There are many paths to wisdom, but one of the most important is learning from our mistakes. It is only through making mistakes that we can learn and grow.

That is wisdom. To err is human, and to forgive is divine.

We have all been there; we have all made mistakes. What if we saw our mistakes as an opportunity to learn and grow? As an opportunity to become wiser?

The world would be a different place if we did. We would be more understanding and compassionate towards others and more forgiving of ourselves. We would view life as a journey full of twists and turns rather than a straight line. We would be more open to new experiences and less afraid of making mistakes. In short, we would be wiser.

This type of wisdom is difficult to acquire because we are constantly bombarded with information that can bias our worldview. And we tell ourselves stories about everything to make it fit into the box, which makes us feel secure.

However, if we can step back and look at the world objectively, we can start to see things as they are. This type of wisdom can be applied in our everyday lives by helping us make better decisions and create a kinder world.

Another philosopher said that "wisdom is in knowing that you don't know nothing." This means that wisdom is not about having all the answers but recognising that there are things that we don't know. This can be a difficult pill to swallow for some people because we live in a society that values knowledge and answers.

However, accepting things we don't know can help us be more open-minded and curious.

And that, my friends, is what I believe to be the true meaning of wisdom that we can grow by:

1. Be curious and ask questions.
2. Be open-minded and willing to learn.
3. Don't be afraid to make mistakes.
4. Take time to reflect on your experiences.
5. Seek out wisdom from others.
6. Practice stillness to observe your thoughts.
7. Don't believe everything you think.

Hope - hopelessness - trust

Why is it hopeless to trust the concept of hope?

The dictionary defines hope as "to desire with expectation of obtainment." In other words, we hope that our desire will come true. But that's a pretty shaky foundation on which to build our lives on.

If we hope our hopes will come true, aren't we just setting ourselves up for disappointment?

As I see it, everything we do not hope will happen, happens. At one point, we become elderly (if lucky), become sick, are laid off, a loved one dies, and experience a lover's grief.

The author, Byron Katie, also has an interesting perspective on hope.

She argues that hope is a form of violence. When we hope for something, we hope that reality will conform to our expectations. We want reality to be how we want it to be instead of how it is. This can lead us to ignore the facts and prevents us from seeing reality.

And that is precisely what makes hope a tricky concept. Hope is based on nothing more than a feeling, meaning it is entirely subjective. What one person sees as a favourable possibility, another may see as a negative likelihood.

This can lead to all sorts of problems, from disappointment and frustration when things don't turn out as we hoped they would, leading to false optimism that prevents us from taking the necessary precautions to protect ourselves from real dangers. In either case, hope is more likely to harm than good.

So, if we stop hoping and instead trust life to unfold just as it is supposed to and trust life to be good whatever comes our way.

Trust is something that we all need in our lives. It's a positive emotion. It allows us to build relationships with others and feel safe in the world. But what is trust, exactly? And how can it help us to live kinder lives?

Trust is our confidence in ourselves, others, and the world around us. It's the belief that things will work out for the best, even when we can't see how they will. Trust gives us the courage to face life's challenges, knowing we can handle whatever comes our way.

When we trust ourselves, we're more likely to act with kindness towards others. We're less afraid of being judged or rejected, so we're more likely to reach out and offer help or support. We're also more likely to listen to our intuition and follow our hearts rather than acting out of fear or selfishness.

Living a kinder life requires stepping out of our comfort zones and into unfamiliar territory. It means taking risks and trusting that things will work out for the best.

There is wisdom in this perspective, and it reassures me that everything will be ok - whatever comes my way.

Try it next time you find yourself getting caught up in Hope Town. Just take a deep breath, bring your attention back to the present moment, and trust that everything will be okay.

Breathe in and relax into whatever is happening right now.

Patience - requires some patience and gratitude

In a world that runs on instant gratification, patience can seem like a virtue of the past. We want what we want, and we want it now.

But as anyone who has tried to hurry a process along knows, rushing rarely leads to positive results. So if patience is a virtue, why is it so difficult for us to practice? And what can we do to become more patient?

One reason patience is hard to come by is that we often believe that being patient means doing nothing. We think of patience as simply waiting for something to happen, but that's not necessarily the case.

Patient people are often also proactive people. They understand that taking the time to do things right often leads to better results in the long run.

Another reason patience is elusive is that we tend to focus on the negatives of a situation. For example, if you're stuck in traffic, you might focus on how late you will be or how frustrated you are. But if you take a step back and look at the situation, you might realize that there's nothing you can do to hasten your commute. In this case, patience isn't about passively waiting; it's about making the best of a less-than-ideal situation.

Here are a few tips to help you cultivate more patience in your life:

1. Shift your perspective from negative to positive.
2. Focus on what you can control.
3. Take small steps instead of big leaps.
4. Practice deep breathing and meditation.
5. Be kind to yourself-patience is a learned skill that takes time to develop!

Patience is not only a virtue but also a key leadership trait. It's the ability to maintain a sense of calm in the face of adversity or to deal with the unexpected. And it's an essential quality in today's workplace where stress levels are high, and there is little room for error.

Here are four ways in which patience can help to eliminate stress in the workplace:

1. Patience allows you to take a step back and assess a situation before taking action. This can prevent you from making rash decisions that you may later regret.
2. Patience allows you to see the bigger picture. When stressed, it's easy to get caught up in the details and lose sight of the bigger picture. By remaining patient, you can keep

your focus on what's important and make decisions accordingly.
3. Patience allows you to build strong relationships. In any workplace, strong relationships are key to success. By being patient with others, you can develop trust and respect, which are essential for any successful relationship.
4. Patience allows you to stay calm under pressure. When things are going wrong, it's easy to panic. But if you remain patient, you'll be able to think more clearly and make better decisions.

There's no doubt that patience is a valuable quality in any leader. By cultivating patience, you can eliminate stress in the workplace and create an environment that is more productive and enjoyable for everyone involved.

Patience is one of the most critical skills a leader can have. It's the ability to stay calm in adversity and keep working towards a goal, even when things go wrong.

Patient leaders show that they're confident in their ability to overcome challenges and willing to persevere, even when the going gets tough. This can be an incredibly attractive quality for followers, who often look to their leaders for guidance and support in times of difficulty.

However, it's important to remember that patience is a skill that must be practiced regularly. It takes time and effort to develop patience, like all skills, but it's well worth the investment.

Leaders who are patient with themselves and others often attract more loyal and dedicated followers. As patience becomes increasingly rare in today's fast-paced world, those who take the time to cultivate this skill often stand out from the crowd.

Gratitude is another essential quality for thoughtful leaders. When leaders are grateful, they show appreciation for the contributions of their followers and make an effort to recognise their efforts. This can go a long way towards building trust and loyalty within a team or organization.

Leaders who express gratitude also send a powerful message that they are interested in their followers' well-being and value their contributions.

This can inspire others to do their best and create a more positive environment. Like patience, gratitude must be practiced regularly to be effective.

Leaders who make an effort to express gratitude regularly often find that they reap the rewards in terms of improved morale and increased productivity from their teams.

We know patience is essential but often find it difficult to practice. How can we cultivate it in our lives?

There are many ways in which we can cultivate patience in our lives. One way is simply to be mindful of the moments when we feel impatient. Then, once we are aware of the feeling, we can take a few deep breaths and remind ourselves that everything is going to be ok.

Another way to cultivate patience is to practice gratitude. When we take the time to appreciate the good things in our lives, it becomes easier to endure the bad times.

Finally, we can see the situation from the other person's perspective. Understanding why someone behaves in a certain way can help us respond with compassion instead of anger.

CHAPTER 13

Wake up and become a philosopher

To be curious is to be a philosopher. It is to look at the world and question why things are the way they are. To be curious is to be alive. When we stop being curious, we stop growing. We become complacent and content with the status quo.

We can't see everything, and we don't know everything. It's what keeps us growing and learning.

We tend to believe that everything vital in our modern world can be counted, measured, and compared. But what if what counts cannot be measured?

We track our steps, calories, money, and time. But are there things that resist being turned into numbers? Things that are more than the sum of their parts?

It's easy to measure things. We can weigh them, count them, or time them. But things are not the same in relations. The number of people in a room differs from the amount of love between them. The height of a mountain is not the same as the sense of awe it inspires.

Some things cannot be captured by numbers alone. And it is these things that truly matter most.

When we believe measuring is the only way to grow people and create new learnings in the organization, we miss something important as we think that only what counts can be measured.

The things that we overlook are learning, relationships and people's capacity to change.

It's not that learning, relationships, and people's capacity to change don't matter; they are just harder to measure. So we focus on what is easy to measure and ignore the things that are hard to measure but matter.

It is why we are constantly surrounded by teachers, regardless of how stupid we believe them to be. Because learning, relationships, and people's capacity to change are continually happening, even if we don't see it.

The Earth School is a learning community based on the belief that everyone has something to teach and something to learn. It is where we can come together to learn from each other and grow as individuals and as a community.

The Danish philosopher Søren Kirkegaard said, "Life can only be understood backwards, but it must be lived forwards." It is what learning is. It's a backwards and forward journey.

First, we look back at what we have experienced to make sense of it, and then we move forwards with a new understanding.

Learning is like being on a spiral staircase. We keep circling, but each time we return to the same spot, we are a little bit higher up and can see things from a new perspective.

It is why learning never really ends. There is always more to understand, more to explore. We are constantly learning every day if we are open to it.

When do we know we have learned something? It is when we can take what we have learned and use it in our lives when we can apply it or put it into practice.

Learning is not just about acquiring new knowledge but about putting that knowledge to use. And when we truly know we have grown new insights, it's also when we can teach others so they also can increase their understanding and become wiser.

It is why learning is so important. It's not just something we do to pass the time or get good grades. Learning is a fundamental part of what it means to be human. We are here on Earth to learn, grow, and contribute our unique gifts to the world and make it better.

It takes one to know one!

A famous saying goes, "you can't love someone until you love yourself." What does this mean? We cannot give others what we do not have within ourselves. If we're not in a place of self-love and acceptance, we will only be able to see our partner as a reflection of our insecurities.

We'll project our baggage onto them and treat them in a way that reflects how we feel about ourselves.

That's not to say that all relationships need to start from a place of self-love, but it is something to be aware of.

What are we looking for in the other person to lead a good life?

One way to think about this is to imagine that each of us is a window. We look out at the world and want to be seen and recognised by others.

In a good relationship, we can see ourselves reflected in the other person. We feel known and understood. It leads to a sense of connection and intimacy. We feel safe to be ourselves and we can explore our world together.

Relationships are vital to a good life because they give us a sense of connection, support, and love.

If we learn to love and accept ourselves, we will be better equipped to handle the ups and downs of a relationship. We will be more likely to see our partner as a separate individual with their own needs and wants rather than an extension of ourselves. Ultimately, this will lead to a more fulfilling and satisfying relationship.

Our relationships with some people always stay the same regardless of how long there can be between seeing one another.

You feel they see you as you are, and you see them as they are, so in some manner, you meet yourselves meeting the other. It's as if you are two columns of a balance scale; each time you get together, the scale is recalibrated.

It's interesting to think about how our perceptions of ourselves change over time. As kids, we might believe that we're invincible and can do anything we set our minds to. As we get older, we might start to doubt ourselves more and focus on our shortcomings. Or, we might come to realize that the person we thought we were isn't really who we are at all.

In any case, it's important to remember that our sense of self is always evolving. Just because we made a mistake in the past doesn't mean we're doomed to repeat it. And just because we don't yet know who we want to be doesn't mean we're lost.

The beauty of life is that we always have the potential to grow and change. So, regardless of who you believe yourself to be right now, know that you have the power to shape your own destiny.

People need to fully understand who they are because our sense of self constantly changes like everything else. We are never the same person twice, continually growing and learning new things about ourselves.

The only way to know who you are is to be aware of yourself as the observer meeting people. By doing this, you can start to see yourself more objectively and get a better understanding of who you are.

There will always be parts of yourself that you don't understand, but that makes life enjoyable. So embrace the mystery and learn to love yourself for who you are, even if you don't fully understand who that is.

The blind spot

We all have blind spots - areas where we are unaware of our biases and assumptions. As a result, we can sometimes unintentionally act in ways that are harmful to others.

For example, a person might make a sexist joke without realizing it is offensive. Or a company might produce a product that is damaging to the environment because it did not consider the total environmental impact of its actions.

However, there is a way to become aware of our blind spots and work to correct them. The first step is recognition.

We must be open to the possibility that we may have biases we are unaware of. Then, we can actively seek out perspectives that differ from our own.

It can be done by talking to people with different backgrounds and experiences, reading books and articles from various sources, and listening with an open mind.

Finally, we must be willing to change our beliefs and actions in light of new information.

By taking these steps, we can correct our blind spots and become more effective members of society.

While our blind spots can be a source of frustration, they can also catalyse positive change. Recognising our blind spots can open our minds to new perspectives and possibilities.

It can challenge the status quo and help us to see the world in new ways. And it can lead to innovation and progress in our lives and the world around us.

Here are three examples of how recognised blind spots can create a better life:

1. In medicine, recognising a blind spot can lead to new treatments and therapies that save lives. For example, doctors have been unaware of the importance of sanitation and cleanliness in preventing disease for centuries. But recognising this blind spot led to

the invention of modern sterilization techniques that have transformed medicine and saved countless lives.
2. In business, recognising a blind spot can lead to new products or services that improve people's lives. For example, when Apple recognised the blind spot of music lovers who wanted to carry their music with them on the go, they created the iPod, revolutionizing the way we listen to music.
3. In our personal lives, recognising a blind spot can help us to overcome challenges and achieve our goals.

For instance, many people struggle with unhealthy eating habits because they're unaware of the nutritional value of foods or the impact that diet has on their health. But when we recognise this blind spot, we can make changes that lead to better health and well-being.

So next time you are frustrated by a blind spot, remember that it might be the key to unlocking something extraordinary.

CHAPTER 14
Follow your intuition

Intuition is often thought of as a gut feeling or a hunch. That little voice inside your head tells you whether something is right or wrong.

But what is it? And how can we develop a stronger sense of intuition?

Philosopher Immanuel Kant believed that intuition was a faculty of the mind that allowed us to grasp the truth without resorting to reasoning.

For Kant, intuition is basic knowledge that doesn't come from the senses or reason. Instead, it's a direct, immediate awareness of something. It means that when we are intuitive, we don't need to think about it or figure it out—we just know it. It might sound vague, but Kant believed that our ethical decision-making depends on this knowledge.

When faced with a moral dilemma, he thought, we need to intuit the right thing to do. Otherwise, we could never be sure that our actions are genuinely ethical. So while gut feelings may come and go, Kant's idea of intuition is much more profound and lasting. It's a way of knowing that can help us make the right choices, even when things are tough.

It may explain why we sometimes have a strong intuitive sense about something even if we can't quite put our finger on why.

For example, you might suddenly sense that you should turn left at the next intersection without knowing why.

Gut feelings, on the other hand, are emotive reactions that arise from our values and beliefs. For example, you might get a sinking feeling in your stomach when you see someone being bullied.

It's essential to distinguish between intuition and gut feelings because they serve different purposes.

Intuition is awareness without thinking, while gut feelings are emotional reactions from the subconscious mind.

Here are four examples that highlight the difference between the two:

1. Intuition is often described as a "knowing" or a feeling that something is true, even if you can't explain why. Gut feelings, on the

other hand, are more like an emotional response to a situation.
2. Intuition is usually straightforward and unambiguous, while gut feelings are often more confusing and hard to pinpoint.
3. Intuition is based on analysis of past experiences and patterns, while gut feelings are more instinctive and come from the subconscious mind.
4. Intuition is usually helpful in making decisions, while gut feelings can sometimes lead to bad decision-making.

In general, intuition is more rational and helpful, while gut feelings are more instinctive and emotional. However, both can be useful in different situations.

As a rule of thumb, intuition is typically associated with positive feelings (e.g., confidence, excitement, etc.), while gut feelings are often negative (e.g., anxiety, dread, etc.).

It is said that intuition always comes from a place of love, while gut feelings are usually rooted in fear. Therefore, intuition will never lead you astray, but gut feelings can often be misleading.

It's about right and wrong!

We all want to be right. It feels good to be right, to know that we are correct. And so we often find ourselves insisting on being right, whether it is in an argument with a friend or family member, or simply in our own heads as we convince ourselves that our way is the best way.

But what if we were not so driven by the need to be right? How would our relationships change? How would we view the tasks we are in charge of?

Either we could be more open to other people's perspectives and be more willing to compromise. Or we could be more flexible in our thinking, willing to try new things and experiment with different approaches.

Whatever the case, it is worth considering whether the need to be right is always beneficial or if there are better things to focus on that can make us feel even better.

For one, the ego would not get in the way as much. We would be more open to hearing others' perspectives and learning from them, even if it meant that we were wrong.

There would be more HUMILITY and less need to defend our ego. We would also be able to build stronger relationships because we would be more open and vulnerable with each other. There would be more trust and respect. Finally, we would be able to have more fun!

We would be less severe and judgmental of ourselves and others. Life would be a bit lighter.

Here are four reasons why letting go of the need to be right can make you a better person:

1. It can help you to let go of your ego. When we're attached to being right, it's because we're bound to our ego.

We want to prove that we're intelligent, competent, and worth listening to. If we can learn to let go of needing to be right all the time, we can also start to let go of our ego.

2. It can help you to become more open-minded. If you're constantly attached to being right, you're likely closed off to new ideas and perspectives. But if you can let go of that attachment, you can become more open-minded and receptive to new ways of thinking.

3. It can help you to become more compassionate. When we're attached to being right, we tend to judge others for their wrong beliefs. But if we can

let go of that attachment, we can start to see people for who they are, with all their flaws and mistakes. We can begin to feel compassion for them rather than being judgmental.

4. It can help you live in the present moment. One of the biggest reasons people mentally suffer is because they're living in the past or the future.

If you're constantly attached to being right about something that happened in the past or anxious about being right in the future, then you're not living in the present moment.

But if you can let go of that attachment, you can start to experience life as it is happening, moment by moment.

Overall, letting go of the need to be right all the time can help us in so many ways.

It can help us to let go of our ego, become more open-minded and compassionate, and live more fully in the present moment.

So next time you find yourself getting wrapped up in needing to be correct, remember these four benefits and let it go.

Afraid of living

Mark Twain, the author, once said, "Let us live so that when we come to die, even the undertaker will be sorry."

Why are we so afraid of dying? Is it the heart-wrenching goodbyes? The not knowing what comes next? Or is it simply the fear of the unknown?

Whatever the reason, this fear can consume us and prevent us from truly living.

How can we let go of this fear and start living?

Here are four ways:

First, try to see death as a natural part of life. Everything born will one day die - it is the cycle of life. Accepting death can help us see life's beauty and appreciate every moment we have.

Second, remember that we are all connected. Although our physical bodies may die, our energy lives on. We are all made up of the same energy, so we are all eternal.

Third, trust that a kind universe will take care of us. When we let go of our fears, we open ourselves up to receive guidance and support from the universe.

Finally, focus on what matters. Instead of worrying about death, focus on living a good life. Be kind, honest, and present- these things will ultimately matter.

When we let go of our fear of dying, we can finally start living.

I have been unconsciously afraid of dying because of my twin brother's death when we were almost 23 years old. I understood this when I met some interesting people in three different places in the world, who enlightened me with the message that I would become very old. And my encounters with the three persons I will share with you here.

Years ago, of all the places, I might have met an angel at Macy's in New York . I was standing in a queue waiting to pay and suddenly this gorgeous fur-clad woman was standing next to me, looking intensely at me. She exclaimed; There's an old soul in you!

Okay, I managed to look around to see if there was a hidden camera, after which the woman asked me if I knew what a shaman was. Of course, I answered in the affirmative. She then continued and told me that I would get very old. After which her mobile rang, and she disappeared with the words; I'll be back!

FOLLOW YOUR INTUITION

New York is New York, and the world is full of colourful souls. I did not think about that experience until a few years later in China. I was on a business trip in Central China and spent a Sunday in a small old town in the company of my Chinese employee, Hui. We strolled around the ancient alleys, and suddenly this elderly and tall Chinese Taoist monk stood in front of us and insisted that we go with him because he had something to tell me.

Hui translated and thought it wise to follow him. We accompanied him in and out of a jumble of tiny streets and alleys until we reached a small house furnished with books and beautiful calligraphy. The monk looked in a little old book after he had studied my forehead and ear (once again, I was secretly looking for a camera). He told me that I would become very old and that Hui should not expect to get quite that old! He gave us an exotic fruit and said we should share it, after which he thanked us that he had been able to deliver his message.

One Monday morning in Copenhagen, I was waiting for the bus to a meeting. This man with a funny high hat was standing and looking at me. I sent him a Mette smile, as it's always nice to start a Monday morning with some good karma. Then, on entering the bus, he turns to me and tells me that

I will get very old, after which he thanks me and moves away.

Now I'm starting to sense that the universe has been so kind as to tell me that even though I lost my twin brother at a very young age, I do not have to be afraid to dying young.

These experiences do not fit into a rational explanatory framework, but I have chosen to use them to let go of my unconscious fear of dying young. Now I can concentrate on living and unfolding my life.

Sometimes we meet the right people at the right time who hand us the missing link so we can move on with our life more easily.

CHAPTER 15
Life and quantum physics

Quantum physics studies the behaviour of matter and energy at atomic and subatomic levels. It is considered one of the most complex and challenging fields of physics and has led to the development of technologies like lasers and transistors and provided scientists with a greater understanding of the universe at its most minor level.

Some of the most famous scientists who have used quantum physics to further their understanding of nature include Albert Einstein, Niels Bohr, and Max Planck. One of the fundamental concepts of quantum physics is that everything is made up of energy. It means that everything in the universe — including us — is vibrating at a particular frequency.

Every thought, action, and emotion creates a corresponding vibration that radiates out into the world. This vibrational energy also interacts with other global energies, including other people's. In other words, our vibrational energy constantly affects everything and everyone around us.

It might sound abstract, but there are many concrete examples of how our vibrational energy affects our lives and the lives of others. For instance, when we smile at someone, we send out positive vibrations that can brighten their day. Similarly, when we get angry or upset, those negative vibrations can negatively affect others when we get angry or upset.

In short, everything in the universe is connected through vibrational energy. What we put out into the world comes back to us — for better or worse. So it's essential to be aware of our thoughts, emotions, and actions, as they can profoundly impact our lives and those around us.

Being human and having pure energy

It's fascinating to think about how everything in the universe is made up of energy. And according to quantum physics, this energy is always in motion. It means that everything is constantly vibrating - including our thoughts and feelings. So, can quantum physics help us to understand the human mind?

There are some intriguing parallels between the two. For example, both quantum physics and the human mind deal with uncertainty. In quantum mechanics, particles can exist in multiple states simultaneously - they're not entirely "defined" until they're observed. Similarly, our thoughts and feelings are often in flux, changing from moment to moment.

Another similarity is that quantum physics and the human mind are non-linear - meaning that cause and effect don't always happen in a straight line.

In quantum mechanics, particles can influence each other even when not physically close. Similarly, things outside our conscious awareness can profoundly affect our thoughts and feelings.

While we still have a lot to learn about quantum physics and the human mind, it's fascinating to think about how they might be related. One day we can use quantum physics to better understand the workings of the human mind.

Carl Gustav Jung, the famous Swiss psychiatrist, proposed that the spiritual mind can see beyond the physical world and tap into a higher level of reality.

This higher level is what he called the "collective unconscious." We can connect with more profound wisdom and understanding by accessing the collective unconscious.

Carl Jung believed that our thoughts and feelings could influence the behaviour of subatomic particles. He was convinced that everything is made up of energy and that our thoughts and emotions can interact with this energy to produce observable effects. He called life an energy process.

Quantum physicists later developed the idea and found that our observations can influence the outcome of experiments.

While it may seem far-fetched, there is evidence to support this theory. For example, in the famous double-slit experiment, electrons behave differently when observed. This suggests a connection between our minds and the physical world. Everything is energy, including our thoughts.

Our thoughts are frequencies that interact with the physical world. When we focus on something, we effectively shine a light on it. The light of our attention can influence the behaviour of particles.

It suggests that we are genuinely connected to the physical world. The double-slit experiment is just one of many experiments that indicate the power of our minds.

LIFE AND QUANTUM PHYSICS

As we continue to explore the nature of reality, it is becoming increasingly clear that our thoughts and intentions can have a tangible impact on the physical world. It means that everything may be connected and subject to the laws of cause and effect.

If we want to change our lives, we must start by changing our energy and thoughts. While we may not yet fully understand how it works, there is no doubt that our thoughts and feelings can have a real and measurable impact on the world around us.

In other words, quantum physics and the spiritual mind may be two sides of the same coin.

Dalai Lama and science

One of the central tenants of Buddhism is that everything is interconnected. It means that everything in the universe is connected at a fundamental level. The Dalai Lama elaborates on this idea in his book, 'The Universe in a Single Atom'.

He argues that everything is made up of energy and that this energy ties everything together. He says everything in the universe is ultimately made up of the same atoms. It means that the universe is, in a sense, contained within every atom. This atomic view of the universe helps to explain why everything is interconnected; it is because everything is literally made from the same stuff.

In short, the universe is in a single atom because everything is made from the same particles. The way these atoms are arranged determines the properties of each thing in the universe, but at a fundamental level, everything is made up of the same building blocks. It helps to explain why everything is connected; it all comes down to fundamental physics.

If everything is energy, then everything is connected. When we act with kindness and compassion, we emit positive energy into the world.

This positive energy has a ripple effect, touching many people's lives. In this way, the Dalai Lama teaches us that our actions matter and that we have the power to make the world a better place.

Dalai Lama has spoken about how he believes quantum physics can help us to understand the concept of emptiness.

He argues that the concept of emptiness (or "sunyata") can be understood by looking at the world at the quantum level. At its most basic, quantum physics tells us that there is no such thing as a solid object; everything is made up of tiny particles constantly moving and changing. In other words, everything is in a state of flux.

By understanding this, we can see that everything is empty of any real substance. However, if we feel anxious or stressed, we may see the same sunset as threatening or ominous.

Our thoughts, feelings, and actions are all made up of energy. And this energy interacts with the world around us, shaping our reality.

For example, you're more likely to see the world as hostile if you're angry. Conversely, if you're happy, you're more likely to see the world as a friendly place.

Our perceptions are not reality itself, but our mental states influence them. Therefore, we must be aware of our thoughts and emotions to create a more positive reality for ourselves.

From this perspective, it is clear that how we view the world plays a significant role in shaping our lives. Therefore, if we can change our perspective and see ourselves and the world around us more positively, this will positively impact our lives.

CHAPTER 16

What you don't know about the brain

According to Lisa Feldmann Barrett, brain research has traditionally been focused on understanding specific areas and functions.

One of the fascinating things about this research is that it challenges traditional ideas about how the brain works. For example, we used to think that the brain was like a computer, processing information linearly.

However, Feldmann Barrett's research suggests that the brain is more like an orchestra, with different regions working together dynamically.

However, her work has shown that the brain is constantly trying to balance its resources, which she refers to as a "budget."

It means the brain is always seeking ways to conserve energy and resources. One way it does this is by making predictions. The brain uses past experiences to predict what will happen next, which helps it save energy by not having to process everything from scratch all the time.

Additionally, the brain is also good at filling in gaps. If information is missing, it will try to fill in the blank using whatever it knows about the world. It can often lead to errors, but it can also be helpful when trying to make sense of something new.

Finally, the brain is constantly trying to simplify things. It allows us to focus on what is most important and ignore distractions.

By understanding these three insights, we can understand how the brain works and why it sometimes makes mistakes.

When we encounter something new, our brain has to decide: do we need more neurotransmitters to deal with this unique situation, or can we get by with what we have? It explains why we sometimes feel overwhelmed by new experiences: our brain is simply trying to figure out how to best deal with the situation and may not have enough resources to do so effectively.

Fortunately, our brain is very good at learning from experience and quickly adapting to new situations. With each new experience, it becomes better at predicting what's coming next and adjusting its neurotransmitter levels accordingly. As a result, we become more resilient over time and able to cope better with whatever life throws at us.

The brain is guessing

Everything we see is coloured by the brain's "budget" or "act" system. The brain makes predictions based on past experiences to generate a picture of the world that makes sense.

However, sometimes these predictions need to be more accurate, leading us to believe things that are false. For example, we may mistakenly see a stationary object as moving if the brain predicts it should be moving based on our experience with similar things. Or, we may believe something is true even though it isn't, simply because the brain has generated a picture we believe in.

While this can lead to some misconceptions, it allows us to see the world more flexibly and fluidly.

By understanding how the brain makes predictions, we can better understand why we see and believe what we do.

The brain is always trying to reduce cognitive load, so we often don't see things as they are. Instead, we see what our brain wants us to see - usually based on what is easiest or what will save the most energy.

It can lead to all sorts of problems, especially in decision making. However, it's important to remember that the brain is just trying its best with the available resources. By understanding how the brain works, we can work around its quirks and make better decisions.

We construct our emotions

Our emotions are more complex than we think. Dr Lisa Feldman Barrett's research proves that our brain constructs emotions instead of just responding to the situation. For example, the amygdala is responsible for the "fight or flight" response. The hypothalamus regulates things like hunger, thirst, and body temperature. And the prefrontal cortex is responsible for higher-level thinking, including emotional regulation.

So how does the brain construct emotions? In a nutshell, it uses past experiences to generate predictions. These predictions are based on three things:

1. the physical sensations we're experiencing at the moment.
2. the thoughts and beliefs we have about those sensations.
3. how we learned to respond to similar situations in the past.

This process constantly happens in the background, allowing us to feel emotions like happiness, sadness, anger, fear, and love. It's also what enables us to feel more than one emotion at the same time. So the next time you're overwhelmed by your feelings, remember that it's not necessarily the situation causing them.

It's your brain that is doing its best to keep you safe and happy. And the best defence against believing a false thought is curiosity. So if you feel down for no reason, take a moment to ask yourself what might be causing that emotion. Chances are, you'll find that your brain is just trying to protect you from something that isn't there.

According to Katie Byron, the best defense against believing a false thought, is curiosity. But what exactly does that mean? And how can we use curiosity to protect ourselves from falling prey to false beliefs?

First, it's essential to understand that the brain constantly constructs emotions based on the information it takes. It is why we may sometimes react emotionally to something even though we know, logically, that there's no reason to. The brain is doing its best to make sense of the world based on its available information.

One way to protect ourselves from false beliefs is to ensure that we're constantly feeding our brains new and accurate information.

The more information we have, the less likely we fall for a false belief. But even more important than that is how we approach new information. If we're open and curious about the world, we're much less likely to believe something simply because it confirms what we already think. On the other hand, if we're close-minded and resistant to new ideas, we're much more likely to accept a false belief simply because it's lazy and easy.

So the next time you feel emotional about something, take a step back and ask yourself: what belief is my brain trying to confirm? Are there other explanations that make more sense? And most importantly, am I open to considering new ideas or shut them out?

You can help protect yourself from false beliefs and emotion-driven decision-making by approaching the world with curiosity instead of scepticism.

Brain versus Mind

The brain and the mind are often interchangeable, but they are different. The brain is a physical organ composed of neurons and other cells. It is responsible for all of the body's vital functions, from breathing to digesting food.

The mind, on the other hand, is an abstract concept. It is where our thoughts and emotions reside. While the brain enables us to have these thoughts and feelings, the mind determines what we think and how we feel. The brain can be seen as a computer, while the mind is the software that runs on it.

Just as a computer cannot function without software, the brain cannot produce thoughts or emotions without the mind. This analogy may seem simple, but it illustrates an important point: without the mind, the brain is little more than a sophisticated machine.

What is the difference between the mind and the brain? It's a question that has puzzled philosophers and scientists for centuries.

And according to Lisa Feldman Barrett, it may be based on a false dichotomy. In her book "Seven and a Half Myths about the Brain," Barrett argues that the mind is not separate from the brain. Instead, she claims the mind is "nothing more than Brain 2.0."

Barrett's argument is based on recent advances in neuroscience, which have shown that the brain is constantly changing in response to experience. This plasticity allows us to learn new skills, form new memories, and make connections between different brain regions. Notably, this process is not restricted to early childhood; we continue to learn and change throughout our lives.

Therefore, if the brain constantly changes, it stands to reason that the mind is continually changing. This theory flies in the face of traditional ideas about the mind as a stable, unchanging entity.

However, Barrett's theory is not without its critics. Some argue that her view of the mind as being nothing more than Brain 2.0, overlooks the vital role of consciousness in our mental lives. Others claim that her emphasis on neural plasticity downplays the role of genes and biology in shaping our minds.

Regardless of whether or not you agree with Barrett's specific arguments, her book offers an intriguing perspective on one of the oldest jokes in philosophy: What's the difference between your brain and your mind?

Echart Tolle, a well-known spiritual teacher, in his book "The Power of Now", explores the difference between the brain and the mind. He explains how the mind is just a tool that the brain uses to process information.

The mind is full of thoughts, emotions, and memories that can trick us into believing that we are our thoughts and feelings.

On the other hand, the brain is the part of us that is aware of our thoughts and emotions. It is the part of us that is aware of the present moment. Tolle gives several examples of how the mind can play tricks on us. For instance, he explains how the mind can make us believe we are our thoughts.

We may have thought about doing something in the future, but that doesn't mean we will. The mind can also make us believe that we are our emotions. We may feel angry or sad, but that doesn't mean those emotions are who we are.

The brain is the part of us aware of our thoughts and emotions, but they do not control it. Instead, the brain allows us to be present at the moment and see things as they are.

However, Tolle believes that the mind is not our true nature. Our true nature is the consciousness that lies beyond the mind. When we connect with this consciousness, we can see the truth about ourselves and the world around us. We are also able to find peace and happiness.

CHAPTER 17

How to train your awareness

If we learn to become more aware, we can train our minds to be more focused and less easily distracted. We can better understand ourselves and the world by focusing on our thoughts and emotions.

Additionally, increasing our awareness can help improve our memory and concentration. It can also reduce stress and anxiety levels. Therefore, there are many benefits to be gained from training our awareness. One way to do this is through meditation or mindfulness practices.

By sitting quietly and focusing on our breath, we can slowly learn to quiet our minds and become more aware of the present moment. With time and practice, we can better understand ourselves and the world around us.

In this chapter, I will show some different ways to become more aware of what's going on in our minds that we may not be aware of. All the exercises and questions will demand stillness to come closer to valuable insights.

Be aware of you watching you

Most of us go through life without considering who is watching us. Instead, we assume we are the only ones observing our thoughts and actions. However, as Michael A. Singer points out in his book 'The Untethered Soul', someone else is always watching us - our higher self.

Our higher self is the part of us aware of our thoughts and actions but is not limited by them. It means that we always have the potential to see ourselves from a higher perspective.

Fortunately, there are ways to become more aware of our higher self. Singer suggests two exercises that anyone can do to begin the process of awakening.

The first is to become aware of our thoughts and emotions as they arise, without judging or attachment. It will help us see that we are not our thoughts or emotions but our observers.

The second exercise is to imagine ourselves in different situations and notice how our higher self would react. For example, we might imagine ourselves in a situation where we are being criticized. Notice how your higher self would respond to this situation- with compassion and understanding or with anger and defensiveness?

By becoming more aware of who is watching us, we can move beyond our limited perspective and into a more expansive way of seeing ourselves and the world around us.

One of the fascinating things we can do is watch our thoughts. It's incredible to think that everything we feel, every single emotion and experience, arises from the thoughts we have in our minds. And yet, our thoughts often feel so accurate and true, as if they are beyond our control.

The fact that we can observe our thoughts means that we have the power to choose what we think about. We can decide whether to give it strength by being attached to it whenever we notice a thought, or we can choose to let go of it.

We are not at the mercy of our thoughts; we can choose what to think about and let go of thoughts that don't do us any good. And what we think about creates our feelings, shaping our reality, as I have mentioned many times.

Start watching your thoughts more carefully. Become aware of your thoughts throughout the day. Then, when you think, take a step back and observe the thought dispassionately. Don't judge or try to change it; just let it be.

Then choose one thought each day that is particularly troubling or negative and then reframe it more positively or neutrally. For example, if you think, "I'm such a failure," you could reframe it as "I'm doing the best I can."

Your thoughts are not necessarily true or real but simply your perceptions. You can learn to control your thoughts and create the reality you want with practice.

Meditation

When we think of training our awareness, we often think of mindfulness meditation. Mindfulness is the quality of being present and aware of what is happening without judgment. By cultivating mindfulness, we can become more present in our everyday lives and better deal with challenging situations.

In his book, Full Catastrophe Living, mindfulness expert Jon Kabat-Zinn defines mindfulness as "the awareness that emerges through paying attention on purpose, in the present moment, and non-judgmentally to the unfolding of experience moment by moment."

He explains that mindfulness is not about thinking or doing but rather about being present and aware of what is happening in the present moment.

Exercise

There are many different mindfulness meditation exercises that you can do, but three of the most basic are mindfulness of breath, sounds and mindfulness of thoughts.

To start practicing mindfulness, Kabat-Zinn recommends setting aside some time each day to sit quietly.

To do mindfulness of breath, focus your attention on your breathing and notice the sensations of the breath as it enters and leaves your nostrils. If your mind wanders, bring your attention back to your breath.

To do mindfulness of thoughts, observe your thoughts as they come and go without getting caught up in them or attached to them. Then, again, if your mind wanders, bring your attention back to your thoughts.

To practice mindfulness of sounds, sit or lie in a comfortable position and focus your attention on the sounds around you. For example, listening to traffic, birds singing, or people talking. Then, gently bring it back to the sound if your mind wanders.

These three exercises can help you train your awareness and embrace the present moment.

Questioning what is hard to question

Byron Katie's work is based on a straightforward principle: our thoughts create our reality.

Therefore, if we want to change our lives, we need to start becoming more conscious about our beliefs and changing our thinking and our attachments to our thinking.

It may sound easy, but it can be surprisingly tricky to question our deepest-held beliefs. We often don't realize that we're holding onto false beliefs until someone points them out to us.

Byron Katie's questioning technique is designed to help us identify these false beliefs and release them.

The first step is to write down a belief causing you suffering. Once you've done that, Byron Katie says to ask yourself four questions: is it true? Can you know that it's true? How do you react emotionally and physically when believing this thought? Who would you be without the thought?

The first question is 'Is it true?' followed by 'Can you know that it's true?' Once we have established that our beliefs may not be reality-based, we can move on to the third question, 'How do you react? What happens when you believe that thought?' This question, answered in stillness, helps us see the consequences of holding onto our beliefs and how they might affect our lives negatively.

Finally, Byron Katie asks us, 'Who would you be without that thought?'. This question allows us to imagine a life in which our beliefs do not define us and to see the possibility of change.

Answering these questions can be challenging, but it's essential if we want to break free from the limitations of our beliefs. It starts with us becoming aware of our false beliefs.

In her book, "How Emotions are Made," neuroscientist and psychologist Lisa Feldman Barrett argues that we should think of emotions as mental constructions rather than objective states of being. This may sound like a slight distinction, but it has profound implications for how we view ourselves and the world around us.

If we think of emotions as subjective states, it becomes much easier to see them as mere products of our thoughts and beliefs. This, in turn, can lead us to question our assumptions and examine our beliefs more critically. After all, if our emotions are just products of our minds, then they are not as infallible as we often assume.

Asking ourselves three simple questions can help to foster this kind of critical thinking:

Exercise

- What am I feeling right now?
- Second, why am I feeling this way?
- Third, is there another way to interpret this situation?

We can think more clearly and make better decisions by adopting a more questioning stance towards our emotions.

Become a truth seeker

We're less likely to question something when we feel sure about it. That sense of certainty can feel comforting, but it can also lead us down a rabbit hole of confirmation bias, where we only seek information that reaffirms our beliefs.

On the other hand, when we approach life with a sense of uncertainty, we're more likely to be open-minded and curious. We're more likely to explore different viewpoints and consider multiple perspectives. And as it turns out, this uncertainty can lead to greater clarity of thought.

In her book, "How Emotions are Made," I love to refer to Lisa Feldman Barrett argues that uncertainty is essential for clear thinking. She writes, "Only when our brain is uncertain does it engage in flexible, creative thinking."

Certainty creates what Barrett calls "rigid categories" in our brains categories that don't allow for much flexibility or nuance. This can lead us to see the world in black-and-white terms and to make snap judgments based on our existing beliefs.

So next time you feel stuck, try approaching the situation with curiosity and uncertainty. It helps you to think more clearly.

Here are three questions you can ask yourself to examine your beliefs:

Exercise

- First, what evidence do I have to support my belief?
- Second, what would be true for my belief to be false?
- Third, what alternative explanations could there be?

CHAPTER 18
Stories to reflect upon

Life is full of stories. Some are happy, some are sad, and some are just plain funny. Some stories also linger in our minds long after they've been read or heard. Stories resonate with us deeply because they contain truths we recognise in ourselves and can feel. In a way, they function as mirrors, reflecting our thoughts and feelings.

We may not always like what we see in these stories, but they can offer valuable insights into who we are and how we want to live our lives. So the next time you come across a story that speaks to you, take a moment to reflect on its message. It might help you to see yourself in a new light.

In this chapter, I will share some short stories you can ponder alone or with your colleagues. I have added questions to each story that help you start wondering how the story reflects something in you and the story you tell yourself.

How Christian gained a less stressful life

Christian's mind raced as he sat in his office chair. All around him, he saw people who were stressed and unhappy. He had been at the company for years and things only worsened. His thoughts about the world, his spouse, his boss and his employees drove him crazy.

One day in the middle of a minor mental power nap, he got this epiphany that thoughts were coming and going, and when he believed in them, he felt stressed, and when he didn't, he was ok. This revelation gave Christian a new perspective on life. Suddenly, all of the stressors that used to bother him seemed insignificant.

He started to pay more attention to the thoughts that popped into his head positive, some negative, but rather than getting wrapped up in them, he observed them without judgement. Over time, this practice led Christian to become a more content person overall.

Exercise

1. What stressful thoughts do you have? Write each thought down.
2. Examine each thought one at a time to determine whether you can be 100% sure that what you believe about this and that is true.

Are you sure the elephant is blue?

Susan was always an outsider. She never quite fitted in with the other kids and was always sceptical of what they said. While the other kids played tag or role play, Susan read books about science and nature.

One day, when Susan was walking home from school, she passed by a group of kids arguing about what colour the sky was. One kid said blue, one said green, and one said yellow. Susan just laughed and went on her way.

Susan knew the human brain wasn't as reliable as people thought it was. The brain could be tricked into seeing things differently depending on how someone looks at them. For example, the sky could be blue to one person and green to another, depending on their perspective.

Susan also knew that the human brain wasn't made for thinking. The human brain was designed to keep humans alive by scanning the environment for danger and reacting quickly. Thinking took a lot of energy and wasn't necessary for survival.

Despite this knowledge, Susan decided to use her brain anyway. She decided to use her brain to learn more about the world and find ways to make it a better place. Even though the human brain wasn't perfect, Susan knew it was still worth using.

Exercise

- When was the last time you experienced a situation where you thought you and your team were aligned, and then everything went wrong?
- With the story about Susan in mind, could the reason for your project not work out, be that each of you had different thoughts about the tasks?

The smart boss learned something new

The new boss was a smart guy. He had a PhD from one of the best universities in the country, and he was good at solving complex problems. But he had a flaw – he couldn't understand why his employees didn't just do what he told them to do. He would give them clear instructions, but they would still mess up. And then he would get frustrated and start yelling at them.

Then one day, the boss learned an important lesson. He attended a seminar on leadership, where he learned that you need to meet your employees where they are, not where you are. So the next day, instead of giving his employees instructions, the boss asked them how they thought things could be done better. And to his surprise, they had some great ideas!

The boss started implementing their ideas, and his team soon performed much better. They were even outperforming other teams in the company!

Exercise

What is your reality?

- The world is dangerous, and I must always be on my guard.
- The world is a friendly place, and I can trust people.
- There is no reality; we create our realities through our stories.

The tipping point

When I was 35 years old, I did something I'm grateful for every day. I don't know what would have happened if I hadn't done it, but it's a decision that has positively shaped my life.

Now, at the age of 55, I still use the lessons I learned from that experience whenever life gives me lemons.

It all started when my boss called me into his office and told me he was firing me. He said there were no hard feelings, but he didn't think I had what it took to succeed in this company. It was the worst day of my life.

I walked out of his office feeling like a failure. All my friends and family told me how great I was at my job. But I had lost everything instantly. As I drove home, all I could think about was how much money I owed on my credit cards and how I would tell my kids that we were losing our house.

But then something amazing happened. My kids ran up with open arms when I got home and hugged me tightly.

They were so happy to see their dad, regardless of whether or not he had a job. That moment made me realize that no matter what happened in the outside world, nothing else mattered as long as I had them by my side.

The next day, instead of looking for a new job, I started looking for ways to start my own business. With the help of some friends, we launched a new company that ended up being very successful.

And the best part is that now my kids can see their dad working hard and being successful - they're so proud of me!

When I wake up, I often remind myself of what happened on that terrible day I got fired, which proved to be a blessing in disguise.

It's helped me stay positive during tough times and continue chasing after my dreams and building a company that makes a difference in my and all my employees' lives.

Today I'm grateful that my old boss fired me, so I could become the boss in my life.

Exercise

Five years from now, what do you imagine you'll be grateful for, that you did today?

CHAPTER 19

One thought from inner peace

I just became a grandmother, for the first time, to little Hubert.

A beautiful little human, now five months old, is in life without judgment and without a filter that prevents his universal love from reaching everyone in his vicinity. We all carry a love that we cover over the years with layers of stories that make us forget our innermost unique, loving core.

Every single one of us possesses that unshakeable core deep within, so why let our thoughts cloud and overwhelm it?

When we recognize this inner strength, we can stand firm against the chaos of life and approach each day with a generous heart.

Becoming aware of this – and recognizing that we don't need to believe everything we think – can help us to start facing life and the world with curiosity and wonder instead of fear.

It's a beautiful thing about us humans. We have the capacity for reflection, self-reflection, empathy and, not least, our need for meaning, coherence and value. It will help you and me unlock what is within and waiting to come out. When you stop and reflect, you allow your mind to be open to new ideas and what may emerge.

While reading this book, you may have become aware of how what you read leads you to places in your mind like they were guides. My words are not essential but where they take you is paramount.

When you let go of my words and follow where they lead you, you may experience something that touches you, a strong sense of trust that everything is OK.

We all want to be happy, don't we? It's only natural to want to feel contentment and satisfaction. Yet, sometimes it seems like happiness is just out of reach. We may find ourselves questioning who we are and what our life purpose is. We may feel stuck, lost, or uncertain of our next steps. If this sounds familiar, don't worry - you're not alone.

The good news is that within each of us lies the wisdom and guidance we need to get back on track. All we need to do is have the courage to listen.

To find happiness and peace of mind, we must first be willing to look within ourselves. This can be difficult because it requires honesty, courage, and vulnerability.

We may not like what we see at first glance. We may be afraid of what we might find. But if we can push through these initial fears, we will be rewarded with a greater understanding of who we are and what we want out of life.

Self-reflection allows us to get in touch with our authentic selves.

It allows us to connect with our innermost desires and highest aspirations. It helps us see ourselves more clearly - warts and all - so that we can start making the changes needed to create an authentic life.

Part of why self-reflection can be so tricky is because it often leads us into uncharted territory and stories we believe to be true.

Once we start down the path of self-discovery, there's no telling where it might take us. We may leave behind old friends, family members, and jobs that no longer serve us. But, on the other hand, we may end up in new places, doing things we never thought possible. And that's OK!

Most of us go about our lives without questioning the world around us. Instead, we take for granted that our buildings were constructed safely, that the food we eat is nutritious and will not make us sick, and that the people we interact with are honest and have our best interests at heart.

What if everything we believed was a lie? What if our world is an illusion created to keep us trapped in a life of servitude?

While it may sound like the plot in a sci-fi movie, there is evidence to suggest that this may be the case. For example, many of us go through life without questioning why we do what we do. Instead, we get up every day, go to work, come home, eat dinner, and watch TV - rinse and repeat.

Have you ever stopped to think about why you're doing all of this? Unfortunately, if you're like most people, the answer is probably no.

What if there was more to life than just following orders and going through the motions? What if there was a way to break free from this cycle of enslavement?

The first step is to become self-conscious, as I have mentioned several times. How much of what we see and believe is real? And how much is just an illusion we've created in our minds?

It's an interesting question to contemplate. If we're honest with ourselves, we don't know for sure.

Once we become aware of the illusory nature of the world around us that we create through the stories we tell ourselves, we can begin to question everything we see and hear when we feel stressed.

With curiosity and a sincere wish to know the truth, it is possible to escape from this artificial reality and discover the truth about our world, which may not be as terrible as the one we tell ourselves.

All we need is already within ourselves. We need to remember this. And little Hubert is here to remind us he is pure awareness and meets the world without any story and judgements.

Embrace the unknown journey ahead. First, you find the tipping point by questioning the thoughts that create stressful feelings and then you see that your world is more kind than you thought.

And when you know that you don't need to trust everything you believe in when it doesn't feel kind, your chance of writing an exciting and compassionate new chapter in your life story is made possible.

It won't be easy, but it will be worth it. Are you ready to take the first step?

Acknowledgements

I'm filled with immense gratitude towards all I have met over the years.

People who have opened my eyes and illuminated what lies within me because they made me reflect and disagree with me. They've allowed me to tap into the potential in us all, so I can use it to create a meaningful impact on our world and be an agent of positive change.

A special thank to Kristian Bluff for his proof reading and wise feedback on the manuscript, which has refined and strengthened my ideas.

My immense gratitude goes out to my book coach, Malene Bendtsen. She is a true creative genius, and her vision helped bring the professional look of my book alive!

With an abundance of appreciation, I also thank my family - their loving support has enabled every one of my endeavours!

METTE REEBIRK

Literature

Barrett, Lisa Feldman. (2021). *Seven And A Half Lessons About The Brain*. Boston US.: Mariners books.

Barrett, Lisa Feldman. (2018). *How emotions are made: The Secret Life of the Brain*. New York, US.: Mariners Books.

Csikszentmihalyi, Mihaly. (2008). *Selvets udvikling: Evolution, Flow og det gode samfund*.: Dansk Psykologisk Forlag.

Dalai Lama, *The Universe in a Single Atom: The Convergence of Science and Spirituality"*. Morgan Road Books, New York, 2005

George, Mike. (2007). *7 AHA-oplevelser: som befrier dig fra stress* (2. udgave). UK.: Borgens Forlag

George, Mike. (2015). *Mindsets: Change your **perceptions** create new **perspectives** and cultivate greater **clarity***. Dubai, UAE.: Gavisus Media.

Gladwell, Malcolm. (2008). *Outliers: The Story of Succes*. US.: Back Bay Books.

Gladwell, Malcolm. (2005). *Blink: The Power of Thinking Without Thinking*. New York, US.: Back

Bay Books.

Goleman, Daniel. (2013). *Fokus: De skjulte mønstre bag unikke præstationer.* DK.: Gyldendal Business.

Hansen, Christian. (2021). *The Influence Mindset: THE ART & SCIENCE OF GETTING PEOPLE TO CHOOSE YOU.* UK.: Lightning Source UK Ltd.

Harari, Yuval Noah. (2015). *Homo deus: En kort historie om i morgen* (2. udgave). DK.: Lindhardt og Ringhof.

Harari, Yuval Noah. (2018). *21 ting du bør vide om det 21. århundrede.* DK.: Lindhardt og Ringhof.

Katie, Byron. (2002). *Elsk det som er: Fire spørgsmål, der kan ændre dit liv.* DK.: Borgens Forlag.

Katie, Byron. (2007). *Om at forandre sin tankegang og forvandle verden.* DK.: Borgens Forlag.

Møllehave, Johannes. (2008). *Før- og eftertanker.* DK.: KRISTELIGT DAGBLADETS FORLAG.

Møllehave, Johannes. (2009). *Det ender godt: Johannes Møllehave Om Døden.* DK.: KRISTELIGT DAGBLADETS FORLAG.

Neill, Michael. (2018). *Creating The Impossible: A 90-day program to get your dreams out of your head and into the world.* US.: Hay House.

Prætorius, Nadja U. (2007). *Stress: Det moderne traume.* DK.: Dansk Psykologisk Forlag.

Reebirk, Mette. (2018). *Work-Life Crossroads: 50 plus! Time for a career change and more meaningfulness with the proven 3-step legacy model.* DK.: CreateSpace independent Publishing Platform.

Singer, Michael A. (2007). *Den ubundne sjæl: Vejen til det åbne hjerte.* DK.: Borgens forlag.

Werner, Nina. (2020). *Fra selvkritik til self compassion: Lær at behandle dig selv som en ven - og vend lavt selvværd, præstationsstress og depression.* DK.: Forfatteren og forlaget Klim.

Senge, Peter M. Scharmer, C. Otto. Jaworsky, Joseph. Flowers, Betty Sue. (2004). *Skabende nærvær - Om nutidsforståelse og fremtidsvisioner.* DK.: Forlaget Klim.

Goleman, Daniel. Boyatzis, Richard. Mckee, Annie. (2002). *Følelsesmæssig Intelligens I Lederskab.* (2. udgave). DK.: Lindhardt og Ringhof.

Varela, Francisco J., & Rosch, Eleanor & Thompson, Evan *The Embodied Mind. Cognitive Science and Human Experience.* The MIT Press 1992

About the Author

Mette Reebirk brings to her audiences insight, understanding and inspiration as she speaks on emotional intelligence, leadership development and conscious living.

From executives looking for the next level of success in their careers to individuals seeking a more fulfilling life, Mette is captivated by the knowledge that can transform leadership and lives for the better.

Her former book "Work-life crossroads" provides invaluable guidance through today's ever changing working environment – don't miss out!

For more information about Mette Reebirk, visit:

www.reebirk.dk

https://www.linkedin.com/in/mette-reebirk/

www.ingramcontent.com/pod-product-compliance
Lightning Source LLC
Chambersburg PA
CBHW031534210526
45464CB00016B/1552